BRAZILIAN MS

FOR DRUMSET

BY DUDUKA DA FONSECA AND BOB WEINER
TRANSCRIPTIONS BY JOHN RILEY

Stream or download the audio content for this book.
To access, visit: **alfred.com/redeem**
Enter the following code: 00-MMBK0009CD_554455

alfred.com

ISBN-10: 0-7692-0987-4
ISBN-13: 978-0-7692-0987-6

EDITOR **DANIEL THRESS**
COVER AND BOOK DESIGN **JACK WALTRIP**
MUSIC ENGRAVING **BOB SHERWIN**
INTRODUCTION **EMILY MOOREFIELD**

RECORDED BY DAVID SARDI/DESSAU STUDIOS, NYC
REMIXED BY DOUG EPSTEIN
POSTPRODUCTION DOUG EPSTEIN, ROGER TALLMAN
AND BOB BURKE

ACKNOWLEDGMENTS

The authors would like to thank Dan Thress for his valuable and heartfelt contributions; John Riley for his meticulous transcriptions and musical advice; Emily Moorefield for her photographs and introduction; Jack Waltrip for his artistic contributions and help with bringing this project together; Bob Sherwin for his engraving expertise and patience; Paul Siegel and Rob Wallis for funding this project; Edilberto Mendes for his gracious help with the photographs; Maucha Adnet for her Brazilian insight and helpfulness; Dom Salvador for his inspiration and knowledge; Arnaldo De Souteiro for his research and help with the pictures; Paul Socolow for his help with the discography; the staff and faculty of Drummers Collective for their support and encouragement; and finally, the musicians who participated on the recording: Café, Maucha, Jay, Romero and Nilson.

In Brazil we have many different rhythms, and in this book we show some of these rhythms. It should be noted that these are my personal interpretations of these particular rhythms based on my musical experiences in Brazil and New York. When you become familiar with the roots of these rhythms, I encourage you to develop your own personal approach to playing Brazilian music. But remember, always respect the *foundations* of the rhythms.

This book is dedicated to my wife Maucha and daughter Alana.

I would like to give special thanks to my teachers Joel Rothman, Sonny Igoe, Keith Copeland, Frank Malabe and Neil Clark, as well as a very special thanks to my parents Hyman and Shirley Weiner.

MUSICIANS

Batucada

Edison Da Silva (Café)	Pandeiro, Repique, Whistle, Tamborim
Duduka Da Fonseca	Surdos, Cuica, Ago-go, Caixa (snare)
Maucha Adnet	Ganza, Tamborim
Jay Ashby	Trombone

Baião and Maracatu

Duduka Da Fonseca	Zabumba, Pandeiro, Snare, Triangle, Ago-go Bells, Caxixi

"Live" Music
Trio Da Paz:

Romero Lubambo	Guitar and Guitar Synthesizer
Nilson Matta	Acoustic Bass
Duduka Da Fonseca	Drums

Drum Examples:

All drum examples are played by Duduka Da Fonseca, except those notated (*) after the audio cue, which were played by Bob Weiner. The pandeiro pattern on page 28 was played by Café.

Duduka uses Sonor drums, Zildjian cymbals, and Vic Firth drum sticks.

CONTENTS

KEY

Audio cues (text in grey boxes) have been indicated for the convenience of synchronizing written exercises to the recordings

( ) = optional notes.

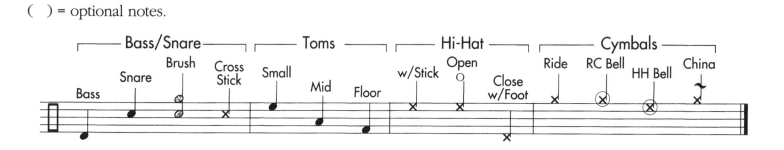

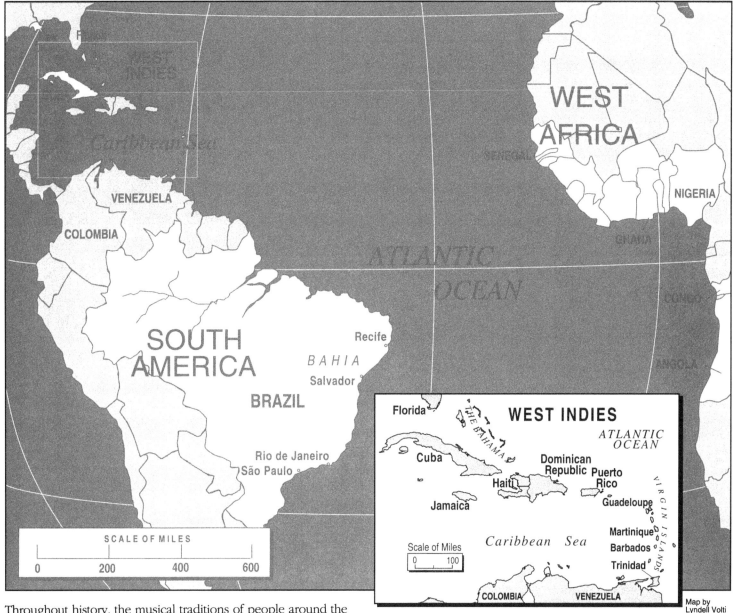

Map by
Lyndell Volti

Throughout history, the musical traditions of people around the globe have come into contact with each other and combined in various ways to create new musical forms. In the United States, South America, and the Caribbean, the influence of African rhythms is particularly strong. Rock, R&B, jazz (United States), bossa nova, samba (Brazil), salsa (Cuba, Puerto Rico, New York City), reggae (Jamaica) and calypso (Trinidad) all have African rhythmic origins. To account for this, we must look at the history of the regions where these forms first began to develop.

The islands of the West Indies and the territory of Brazil were among the first parts of the New World to be colonized by the great European powers—Spain, Portugal, England and France. Originally inhabited by various Indian tribes, these populations were enslaved or eliminated until the Europeans gained control of the areas they wanted and began exploiting agricultural and mineral wealth. To turn such "undeveloped" lands into money-making enterprises required huge amounts of cheap labor. In those days in the Americas, that need was filled by the African slave trade. Slavery brought hundreds of thousands of Africans to the Caribbean islands, South America, and the United States. Most came from West Africa, though many were also taken from central Africa, the region now known as Zaire. Portugal shipped slaves from its colonies Mozambique and Angola in southern Africa to its New World settlement, Brazil.

From the 16th to the 20th century in the colonized regions, Europeans, Africans, and what was left of the Indian populations came together in an immense blending of race, language, religion, social customs—and of course, music. Drumming is an integral part of everyday life in Africa, and the traditions from there were carried on in the Caribbean and Brazil. Music and dance are central in these societies to religious and social ritual, communication, and entertainment. Drums are believed to have spiritual power, power to heal, to "speak," to tap natural forces and affect human energy and emotion. The styles mentioned earlier, and many others as well, use a mixture of African rhythms and European-derived melodies, and instruments from both cultures.

The coming together of these elements in Brazil began in the year 1500 when the Portugese explorer Pedro Alvares Cabral, sailing to reach India, veered too far west of Africa and landed on the northeast peninsula of Brazil. The Portuguese colonization did not begin in earnest for some time, as it wasn't until 1532 that the first permanent settlement was established, at São Vicente in the state of São Paulo. The settlement of the northeast, which would become a vital area both culturally and economically, also began at this time with the founding of the city of Salvador in the state of Bahia in 1539.

5

African slaves began arriving in large numbers in Brazil in the mid-1500s, to meet the demands of the ever-more-profitable and important sugar and mining industries (Indian slaves had been deemed unfit for this type of labor). It has been estimated that by 1798, fully one-half the population was African, including both free blacks and slaves. The majority of Africans settled in the northeast, especially the state of Bahia, which to this day has the largest black population in the country.

It is often said that the music of Brazil evolved from three separate traditions, the European, African, and native or Indian. This is a true but very general statement. Though drawn from these three sources, Brazil's music is extremely varied and the origins of specific forms often unknown. Races and cultures mixed very thoroughly in many respects. Therefore, it is best to think of the development of Brazilian music not in terms of a linear, step-by-step progression but as the result of different musical traditions, mainly those of Portugal and several West African nations, coming into contact with and transforming one another to create new kinds of music.

Much of this new or *Afro-Brazilian* music can be loosely defined as those folk forms which developed in Brazil as a result of various cultural influences but which exhibit strong African traits. It is a large, diverse group of musical forms, many of which are alive and well in Brazil today and are constantly being amended, updated and added-to. Included are a number of old and modern styles whose names also refer to their accompanying dances. The *samba* is the best known of these. Samba is universal in Brazil, where it both reflects and is an integral part of everyday life. To the world, samba is virtually synonymous with Brazil and represents the intense, vibrant nature of Brazilian music. In addition, there are types of music and dance associated with African religious practices, the enactment of christian teaching or historical events, and various ritual competitions, in whose forms the African element is very much the distinguishing characteristic.

The specific contributions of the European, African and Indian traditions to Brazilian music are hard to pinpoint. It is known that Portuguese, and to a lesser extent Spanish and even Spanish-American music (such as the Cuban *habanera*) contributed many of the melodies and melodic forms used in Brazil. Portuguese folk music contains elements that are common to much European music, such as verse-and-chorus song structure, polyphonic singing (multiple harmonizing voices), and the use of stringed instruments. Certain rhythm instruments associated with Brazilian folk music, such as the large double-headed drum called the *zabumba* (or *bombo*, *bumba*, or *tambor grande*), the *caixa* or snare drum, the *surdo*, another large drum, and the *pandeiro* or tambourine, also come from Portugal.

African tradition, on the other hand, largely accounts for the rhythmic aspect of Brazilian music. In the first 200 years of colonization, most Africans who were brought to Brazil as slaves came from Angola or the Congo (Bantu tribespeople); in the later years of the slave trade, the majority of Africans were from Nigeria (Yoruba tribespeople), Benin (Fon people) or Dahomey. The Bantu influence is generally considered to be most apparent in the older forms of secular music, while Yoruba and Fon traditions are evident in religious music and dance. In Brazil, these various forms mixed with each other as well as with Portuguese styles over 400 years of (unwritten) musical history, and so it is difficult to determine the precise source of a given rhythm or style. Two predominant rhythmic features that usually indicate an African source are the syncopated 2/4 meter and the layering of rhythms on top of a regular pulse. Call-and-response singing is a common vocal trait. Many of the rhythm and percussion instruments used in Afro-Brazilian music are of African origin, such as *chocalhos* (rattles and shakers) like the *xaque-xaque*, *ganza*, *afoxe* and *caxixi*; scraper (*reco-reco*); bell (*ago-go*); *atabaque* or single-headed, conga-like drum (also called *tambor*, *ilu*, *tambu*, or *mulemba*); and the *berimbau* or musical bow, an instrument that looks like a bow with a metal string and a gourd attached to the bottom, believed to have originated in Angola. The berimbau functions as both a rhythm and melody instrument and is used to accompany the ritual fight-dance known as *capoeira*.

An instrument whose origin is completely lost in the shuffle between Africa and Europe is the *cuica* (also called *puita*) or friction drum. Though brought to Brazil by Bantu slaves, the cuica had also been known in Portugal and Spain for centuries. It is possibly a Moorish (Moslem African) instrument, although other authorities believe it came from sub-Saharan Africa, where its sound is thought to have been used by hunters in luring lions. Somewhere between a drum and a melody instrument, the cuica has a remarkable pitch range and volume capabilit, and is one of the most distinctive elements of Afro-Brazilian music.

The music of the many Brazilian Indian tribes has not had a pronounced effect on most of the country's popular styles. Certain instruments, however, such as gourd rattles or *maracas* (originally, *mbaracas*) come from Indian tradition. Also, the use of flutes, fifes and piccolos in some rural samba forms may reflect the popularity of these instruments in South American Indian music.

Afro-Brazilian popular or secular music includes older music/dance forms such as the *lundu*, *jongo*, *batuque*, *coco*, *baião* and *maxixe*, and the more modern *samba* and *bossa nova*; religious forms include music from the African *Candomble* cult and the *afoxe*; and among ritual forms are the processional dances known as *congada* and *maracatu* and the

Photo courtesy of Arnaldo De Souteiro

strenuous march-dance called *frevo*, as well as the previously-mentioned *capoeira*. It should be kept in mind that these are examples of only a few of the many styles that developed in Brazil. They are good examples of the cultural blending that characterizes Brazilian music, but are by no means the only styles worth studying.

POPULAR MUSIC

Predominantly African music/dance styles, some of which date back to colonial times, form the basis of much of the Brazilian popular music of

Traditional Samba group

Photo courtesy of Arnaldo De Souteiro

today. The *lundu* was one of the most important of these, and represents some of the first borrowings of African rhythms by European music. It was a mid- to rapid-tempo song/dance performed to the accompaniment of guitars. By the late 1700s, lundu had become a very popular salon entertainment among the upper class of both Rio de Janeiro and Lisbon. A variation called the *corta-jaca* gained favor in the 1800s. Both of these styles were forerunners of the *maxixe* and the modern *samba*.

Of more obvious African origin were the *jongo*, *batuque* and *coco*. Drawn from Bantu tradition and still found in some areas of south and south-central Brazil, jongo is a typically African circle dance performed by men and women moving in a counter-clockwise direction. Jongo songs are known as *pontos* and are sung in a call-and-response fashion, with one or two solo singers being answered by the chorus of dancers. The batuque, from Angola or the Congo, was also a circle dance originally but is no longer performed today except in the state of Sao Paulo, where it is danced by men and women in rows. A distinguishing characteristic of the batuque and many other African dances is the *semba* or *umbigada* (from Portuguese *umbiga*, "navel"), in which the dancing couples touch navels. The word "samba" comes from semba. As with jongo, the batuque was sung in a call-and-response between soloists and dancers. Typically, the songs that accompanied these forms were improvised and either commented on the dance itself (jongo, *pontos de visaria*), community news and gossip (batuque, *modista*), or were songs of aggression, bravado and challenge (jongo, *pontos de desafio*, batuque, *porfias*). The rhythm of the batuque—a basic sixteenth note-eighth note-sixteenth note figure very common in African and Afro-Brazilian dance music—is carried on in modern-day samba which, when it first appeared, was called *batucada*.

Other folk dances from different regions of Brazil also took their forms from African circle dances. Among these are the coco, which originated in the coastal areas of the northeastern states of Ceara, Rio Grande Do Norte, Paraiba, Pernambuco, Alagoas and Sergipe. There were many variations of the coco, but mainly it was a rural dance whose songs were often of the improvisational style known as *embolada*. Cocos were often named after the particular drum or percussion instrument used to accompany them, such as the *coco-de-ganza*.

BAIÃO

The *baião* is a very old rhythmic form which may have come from Arab culture. In Brazil, it developed in the *sertão* or dry interior region of the state of Paraiba. The baião is unusual in that the accordion, a European instrument not usually found in Brazilian music, is part of its traditional ensemble, along with *zabumba*, *pandeiro* and triangle. Baião was introduced to Rio de Janeiro and São Paulo by Luiz Gonzaga in the 1940s, and its rhythm has since been worked into many styles of music, including jazz and fusion, and of course samba, where it produced a hybrid known as *samba-baião*.

SAMBA

The best known of the many Afro-Brazilian music/dance forms is the *samba*. It is popular throughout the whole of Brazil; different regions foster their own variations, but all are of the samba family. The roots of samba, like those of the jongo and batuque, are in Angolan or Congolese round dance. An early version of the samba that was very common in Bahia, the *samba-de-roda* ("round samba"), featured many elements that are still typical of samba today, such as the 2/4 meter with the accent on beat 2, and layers of syncopated rhythms on top, played by an ensemble consisting of drums, tambourine and cowbells.

Outside of Bahia where it was born, samba took hold most strongly in the *favelas* or *morros* (slums) of Rio de Janeiro. The favelas are mainly populated by poor blacks. In the early years of the 20th century, samba as played and danced in Rio began to be recognized as a form of its own, and was referred to as *samba de morro* ("samba of the morros") or *samba batucada*. It was already a major part of the street celebration of carnaval in Rio when the first samba recording was made in 1917. "Pelo Telefone" ("On the Telephone") by Ernesto dos Santos, known as Donga, became a big hit, and samba grew into a national passion, thanks to the latest technology: radio. This was the start of what has since become a yearly ritual in Brazil of recording and promoting sambas composed especially for the carnaval festivities. Each year brings a new batch of *sambas de enredo*, sambas composed for a samba group—one of the many *escolas de samba*—to play in the carnaval parade/competition in Rio. These songs, which are often clever, pointed commentaries on social or political issues, are heard on the radio for weeks before carnaval begins, and the "hit samba" for the year is chosen by popular approval.

It is interesting to note that "Pelo Telefone," though known as a samba, was also very much influenced by the *maxixe*, which had been the popular dance style up to that point. The maxixe was an Afro-Brazilian "take" on European ballroom dances and is said to have been first danced by a man named Maxixe at a carnaval ball in Rio in 1882. By 1915 it was an international craze, although polite society tended to frown on the maxixe as being loud, wild, and shockingly sexual.

The samba as played in Rio for carnaval is marked by the absence of melody instruments. However, a single escola de samba ("samba school," group that performs samba music and dance at carnaval) may include hundreds of drummers and percussionists, known collectively as the *bateria*, as well as many dancers and marchers, and elaborately decorated floats.

The samba bateria consists of the *surdo* or large double-headed drum played using the hand and a beater, of which there are three types: low-, medium-, and high-pitched; the *repinique*, a smaller double-headed drum which can also serve as the internal conductor or leader of the ensemble; the *caixa* or snare drum; the *tamborim*, a single-headed drum about 6" in diameter which is held in one hand and played with a beater consisting of several thin sticks; the *cuica* or friction-drum; the *pandeiro* or tambourine; plus *agogo* bells, which are like different-pitched cowbells; *whistles* to signal changes in the music and assorted types of *ganzas*, shakers.

The best and most popular escolas compete each year in the carnaval parade, performing their specially composed sambas with great energy, passion and gaiety. The escolas are judged on the quality of the music, dancing, lyrics, and performance as a whole, and it is a very great honor to be declared the winner of carnaval. Also known as Mardi Gras (in New Orleans) and celebrated throughout the Caribbean and South America, carnaval originally came from Europe. It is several days of wild merrymaking which in former times, when the church's influence was more pervasive, was the last chance people had to enjoy themselves in this manner before the forty days of Lent (spiritual preparation for Easter) began.

Samba is the lifeblood of Brazilian popular music. It has flourished since the 1920s, accepting and integrating the influence of many other types of music, and producing along the way many notable singers, musicians and composers. Among the pioneers of samba were Ataulfo Alves and Noel Rosa, both brilliant songwriters of the 1930s; pianist Jose Barbosa da Silva, known as Sinho; Moreira da Silva, who performed in the style known as *samba de breque* ("break samba") in which phrases are "scatted" or spoken rapidly during breaks in the music; and composers Alfredo da Roche Viana, called Pixinguinha, and Ari Barroso, who wrote "Aquarela do Brasil," a famous samba. One of Brazil's important classical composers Heitor Villa-Lobos achieved success and recognition in Europe and the United States. Villa-Lobos influenced many great Brazilian musicians including Antonio Carlos Jobim. Ernesto Nazaré was a classical musician that fell in love with the different forms of Brazilian popular music. He was the "bridge" between classical and popular music in Brazil, much in the same way that George Gershwin was in the United States. Other important composers and musicians include Dorival Caymmi, Radamés Gnattali, Garoto, Cartola, Bororó and Chiquinha Gonzaga.

BOSSA NOVA

In the late 1950s, singer/guitarist João Gilberto and composer/arranger Antonio Carlos Jobim "cooled down" the samba and created a form known as *bossa nova*. In its sophisticated arrangements and use of simplified samba feels that were nevertheless intensely rhythmic, bossa nova achieved a level of subtlety and sensuality that had not previously existed in Brazilian popular music. The 1958 release of João Gilberto's album *Chega de Saudade* (*No More Blues*), arranged by Jobim, marked the beginning of the bossa nova revolution in Brazil. The record was an enormous hit, and musicians in other countries began to take notice. A concert in New York's Carnegie Hall in 1962 featuring three of the style's most important musicians— Gilberto, Jobim, and Luiz Bonfa—with American jazz players Stan Getz and Charlie Byrd, introduced bossa nova to the United States. The huge success of singer Astrud Gilberto's version of "Girl from Ipanema" (written by Antonio Carlos Jobim) established bossa nova as an important part of the music of the early '60s both in the U.S. and Europe. Between 1961 and 1963, over a hundred bossa nova albums were released in North America alone.

From its early days, bossa nova made full use of other musical influences, as exemplified by the playing of three important drummers: Edison Machado, who was connected with the jazz scene in Brazil; Milton Banana, whose style was closer to traditional samba; and Dom Um Romao, whose work was strongly in the *Afro* or African-influenced vein. These three musicians paved the way for many other great drummers of Brazilian contemporary music, such as Airto Moreira, Helcio Milito, João Palma and Rubens Barsotti. Other composers and performers who contributed much to the development of bossa nova were João Donato, Marcos Valle, Johnny Alf and Newton Mendonca.

RELIGIOUS MUSIC

Many religious traditions which originated in West Africa and came to Brazil with the slaves are still practiced today, especially in Bahia. *Candomble* is a word used to describe such religious traditions. Analogous to the Caribbean cult known as *Santeria*, Candomble consists of African beliefs and practices which were modified by slaves to accommodate the Catholic teaching forced on them. As practiced today, it includes cults descended from several African sources. The Ketu and Jesha of the Yoruba, the Gege originally of the Fon of Benin, and the Congo-Angola which derives from those two nations are all Candomble cults. In addition, other cults (such as *Umbanda* and *Macumba*) are combinations of African and European spiritual beliefs that are greatly influenced by Candomble and are commonly practiced in Brazil.

The music which accompanies Candomble rites is quite clearly African and may be sung in any of a number of Yoruba, Fon or Congo dialects, or in Portuguese, or a mixture of these. The singing is usually a call-and-response with the soloist and chorus often singing the same melody and sometimes overlapping their parts. Drumming is the most important element of the accompaniment. A typical ensemble consists of three drums, atabaques of different sizes, the largest of which is the *rum*, the medium-sized, *rumpi*, and the smallest, *le*. A shaker or ago-go bell is often used as well. The master drummer plays the largest of the three drums and improvises on the basic rhythm as well as directing or controlling the dance by what he plays. Without exception, the drummers are men.

The drums used in Candomble rituals are considered sacred and are believed to posess a life-force, or *axé*, which is periodically renewed in a special ceremony. Drums are also made holy or blessed for Candomble use by such means as animal sacrifice and the offering of food to the *orixas* (Candomble gods). In Candomble, certain rhythms are assigned to a particular orixa and played for the purpose of calling that spirit to posess one or more of the ritual's participants. In the Ketu cult, the *ajala* rhythm is for Xango (or Shango), god of lightning and justice; the *aguere* rhythm denotes Iansa, a female warrior and wind goddess; and the *igbim* rhythm is played to Oxala or Obatala, king of the gods, the god of creation. Secularized or "street" versions of some Candomble rhythms are contained in the musical styles known as *afoxe* and *afros*, centered in Bahia. Afoxe songs are often sung in the Yoruba language and are also concerned with the Candomble gods, as well as contemporary social issues.

RITUAL AND PROCESSIONAL MUSIC

Parades, processions and dances in which the costumed participants represented characters from African or Portuguese history, or figures from church teaching, were often used by Jesuit missionaries in the colonial period as an entertaining method of Catholic education, and as part of the celebration of religious feast days. This tradition is carried on today in two processional forms, the *congada* and the *maracatu*.

The *congada* combines elements of European folk or street theater with African rhythms. Despite its name, the congada is not an African form. It was (and is) danced by both blacks and whites who "played" characters from the medieval poem *The Song of Roland*, which recounted battles between Europeans and Moors (Moslem Africans). During the days of slavery, a dance re-enactment of the coronation ceremonies of African tribal kings also became part of the congada. The congada procession is accompanied by drumming on atabaques, and also by stringed instruments such as the *viola* (guitar with five sets of double strings) or *rabeca* (fiddle), which come from the Portuguese tradition.

The *maracatu* originated in the city of Recife in Pernambuco, where it is a central feature of the carnaval celebration. Its origins are obscure. At one time a dance-ceremony of the cult of Xango, the maracatu also includes many elements apparently preserved from the coronation rites of African kings, and was performed by slaves in colonial Brazil who had been forced into Catholicism. Thus, the maracatu draws from Candomble, from Christianity, and from African tribal rituals of allegiance and accession to power. The characters of the dance include a king, queen, ambassador and prince. The central figure is the *dama-do-paco* ("court lady"), who carries the *calunga*, a small doll dressed in white which is thought to represent the power of the king or the gods. Rhythms used are specific to various sections or themes of the parade as it moves toward the crowning of the king, and are played on various drums (including the caixa and zabumba), percussion instruments and ago-go bells.

Recife is also home to the *frevo*, a vigorous march-dance in fast 2/4 time. The word "frevo" comes from the Portuguese word *ferver*, meaning heated or fevered. Frevo is a descendent of the *marcha-polka*, a form which in turn came from the *marcha* style of military music adapted for dance use, and the popular and lively polka. It often begins in a row formation, but as the rhythms intensify a circle is formed, with one solo dancer in the middle whose dance-rhythm is syncopated to that of the beat. The rhythms then build to a frenzy, becoming so fast and powerful that the dancers seem to be crazy. Because it is an adapted form of military parade music, the frevo uses many brass instruments, plus drums and percussion.

The ritualized fight-dance known as *capoeira* originated in Angola. While not exactly a cult in the religious sense, capoeira is practiced by members of a "club" who observe special rules and disciplines in performing it. Certain rhythms correspond to particular moves or "strokes" of the dance. It is thought by some to have been created by slaves—a form of martial art masquerading as dance—and can be as deadly as karate. Capoeira was, in fact outlawed for a time on account of its use by gangs in Rio and Sao Paulo in the 1930s and 40s. Since then, its practice has been nonviolent. A combination dance, game and fight performed by two people at a time within a circle of other players (formerly only men, with women being allowed in recently), capoeira requires great skill. It is accompanied by two or more *berimbaus*, small atabaque, ago-go bells, shakers, and pandeiro.

In these and many other forms, Brazilian music continues to fascinate musicians and listeners worldwide. In the 1970s, the great percussionist Airto Moreira brought Brazilian rhythms to the world of jazz and fusion through his work with Chick Corea, Miles Davis, and his own band which included his wife, singer Flora Purim. Also in recent years, Brazilian jazz greats Hermeto Pascoal and Egberto Gismonti, and singers such as Milton Nascimento, Gilberto Gil, Djavan and others have created new mixtures of samba, baião, Afro-rhythms and western pop music. Popular artists such as David Byrne and Paul Simon have made use of Brazilian rhythms and styles in their music as well, bringing them to a wider audience. As we approach the 21st century, the vibrant music of Brazil continues to evolve as one of the truly unique and beautiful traditions of the world.

Emily Moorefield.

Photo courtesy of Edilberto Mendes

The spirit of Carnaval

Photo courtesy of Edilberto Mendes

We would like to dedicate the samba section to the late Edison Machado,
one of the most important and influential Brazilian drummers.
1934 – 1990

BATUCADA BASIC PATTERNS

Low Surdo

High Surdo

Ganza

Snare (Caixa)

Tamborim

Ago-go Bells

Cuica

Pandeiro

Repinique

IMPROVISED

BATUCADA

Batucada is samba played with percussion instruments only.
The rhythm originated with the African dance batuque from
Angola and the Congo. When playing batucada, the percussion instruments are usually as follows:

REPINIQUE (São Paulo) or REPIQUE (Rio de Janeiro)

The repinique is a double-headed drum carried over the shoulder and played with one or two sticks. Its high-pitched sound, similar to the high timbale played in Afro-Caribbean music, is used in small ensembles such as the batucada that was recorded for this tape, to signal cues for beginnings, breaks, endings, etc. In larger samba schools the cues are given with a whistle or with hand signals.

SURDO

Surdo drums are double-headed drums (wood or metal) that range comparatively in size from a floor tom to a bass drum. Surdos are held with a neck strap that positions the drum in front of your body, allowing you to perform in street parades. The drum is played with a soft mallet in the right hand to produce an open tone, and a muffled tone by placing your other hand on the calf or plastic drum head while the mallet strikes the drum.

LOW SURDO

Surdo drums are made in different sizes to create different pitches. The largest surdo produces the lowest tone. Samba is played with a 2/4 feel and pulse—the low surdo plays a muffled or muted note on beat 1 and an open note on beat 2. This pattern could be thought of as, "one—two, one—two," or, "short—long, short—long."

HIGH SURDO

The high surdo is a smaller drum with a higher pitch. The high surdo rhythm features an open tone on beat 1, and a muffled tone on beat 2— "One—two, One—two," or "Long—short, Long—short." This pattern is the opposite of the low surdo part and when played together they create the pulse or heartbeat of samba.

GANZA

Ganza is the name given to a cylindrical metal instrument filled with small stones or pieces of metal which is played by shaking. The rhythm produced by shaking the ganza is usually based on 16th-notes with varying accents. The accented downbeats (beats 1 and 2) are played by pushing the instrument forward and away from your body. The 16th-note pickups going into the downbeats are accented by bringing the instrument toward you. The unaccented notes fall in between the two motions. The phrasing that is created when playing the ganza is often imitated in the snare and bass drum patterns that we will hear later.

SNARE DRUM (CAIXA)

The snare drum that is used in Brazilian ensembles is similar to a piccolo snare drum and is usually 13" in diameter. Like the surdo, the snare drum has a shoulder strap that allows you to walk while playing it. Originally made of wood, most caixa today have metal shells.

The snare drum pattern that is played in our batucada is an important basic samba pattern. The notes are "buzzed" or played as press rolls.

AGO-GO BELLS

Originally from West Africa, ago-go bells consist of two or three different pitched metal bells welded together. As with the tamborim, one hand holds the instrument while the other strikes it with a stick.

There are many different patterns that can be played on ago-go bells. The rhythm that is played on the tape is a simple pattern that helps keep the groove.

TAMBORIM

The tamborim is a single-headed drum, smaller than a tambourine (about 6" in diameter), and without jingles. Tamborim shells can be made of wood, metal or even fiberglass. Due to its small size, the tamborim can easily be held with one hand and struck with a thin wooden, bamboo or fiberglass stick (or two sticks taped together) in the other hand.

The rhythmic patterns that are played on the tamborim are similar to the accents and phrasing of the snare drum pattern. There are many popular tamborim rhythms, some of which we will play on the snare drum in following sections.

CUICA

The cuica is a single-headed drum with a rod connected to the the underside of the drum head. The rod is pulled with a wet cloth, producing friction and creating the sound of the instrument. Pressing down on the top of the head near where the rod is attached will produce higher pitches—releasing the pressure from the head will produce lower tones.

On our tape, the cuica is used to improvise parts or "melodies," rather than playing a specific rhythm.

PANDEIRO

The pandeiro, a tambourine with jingles, is very popular in many different types of Brazilian music. The playing of the pandeiro requires a great deal of skill and technique.

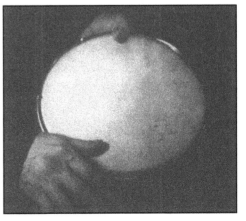

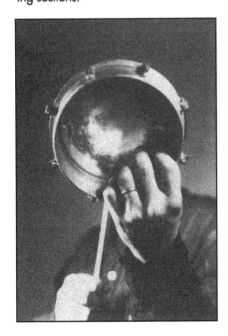

Musical instrument photos by Emily Moorefield

11

We will begin with one of the basic rhythms played by the snare drum section in samba schools. One of the keys to understanding Brazilian music is feeling the pull towards a "triplet pulse" against the 2/4 feel of samba. The examples on the tape will help with the phrasing.

Exercise 1 Snare drum pattern #1

The following snare drum pattern is typically played on the tamborim. The right hand plays all the accents and the left hand "fills in" the other sixteenth-notes.

Exercise 2 Snare drum patterns #2—Tamborim pattern

You can also emphasize the accents in this pattern with rimshots.

Exercise 2a Snare drum patterns #2—Played on the rim

Here is another common tamborim pattern. Notice the slight variation of the accented notes and the new sticking.

Exercise 2b Variation on snare drum patterns #2—Tamborim pattern

On drumset we can use the toms to imitate the sound of the surdos. The left hand muffles the head on the last sixteenth-note of beats 1 and 2, and releases on beat 2 (open tone). The sound of the palm (pickups into the downbeats), are in effect "ghost notes" and are often felt rather than heard. We will start by playing a basic surdo pattern on the floor tom.

Exercise 1 Low surdo part—Basic

Variations:

Exercise 2 Low surdo part—1st Variation

Exercise 3 Low surdo part—2nd Variation

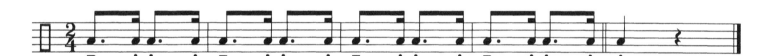

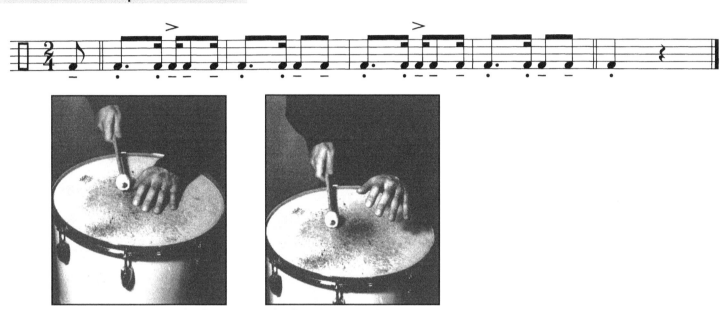

Imitating the surdo on the floor tom. (Left) closed tone; (Right) open tone.

MIDDLE AND HIGH SURDO

The middle and high surdo parts usually alternate with the low surdo. The pattern is the same as the low surdo except that the open and muffled tones are reversed. Try playing the middle surdo part on the middle tom.

Exercise 4 Middle surdo part—On middle tom

Now we will combine snare drum pattern #1, with the basic low surdo part.

Exercise 5 Snare drum pattern #1—With low surdo part

R L R L R L R L

Now we will add the middle surdo part played on middle tom.

Exercise 6 Snare drum pattern #1—With middle and low surdo parts

The high surdo part can be included on the small tom.

Exercise 7 Snare drum pattern #1—With high, middle and low surdo parts

The surdo sequence without the snare drum looks like this:

Exercise 7a Surdo sequence

You can reverse the high and middle surdo parts as follows:

Exercise 8 Snare drum pattern #1—With high, middle and low surdo parts—With middle and high parts reserved

New surdo sequence:

Exercise 8a Surdo sequence

Now we will play different variations in the low surdo part.

Exercise 9 Snare drum pattern #1—With high, middle and low surdo parts with variations

Snare drum patterns 2 and 2a, can also be played with the low surdo part.

Exercise 10 Snare drum pattern #2a—With low surdo part (basic)

Variations on the low surdo part—the left hand plays the snare drum and the right hand plays the floor tom.

Exercise 11 Snare drum pattern #2a—With low surdo part with variations

Now we will add the middle and high surdo parts. The left hand stays on the snare drum and the right hand plays on the toms.

Exercise 12 Snare drum pattern #2a—With high, middle and low surdo parts

"Reverse Surdo"
Some sambas "reverse" the low surdo parts in the first and second measures as follows:

Exercise 13 "Reverse surdo"

The idea of reversing the samba patterns is a concept that we are using to explain how measures 1 and 2, can be reversed by starting the phrase with measure 2. In actual playing situations, samba phrases are determined by the melody or song and are not thought of as "forward" or "reversed."

Next is snare drum pattern 2, with the low surdo part reversed. Again, the right hand plays on the toms and the left hand on the snare drum. Also notice that the snare drum pattern does not start on a downbeat.

Exercise 14 Snare drum pattern #2—With the low surdo part reversed

Now we will add the high and middle parts.

Exercise 15 Snare drum pattern #2—With high, middle and low surdo parts reversed

BASS DRUM AND HI-HAT

We can use the bass drum to keep the underlying pulse much like the surdos. The sixteenth-note phrasing is the same as the first snare drum exercise (snare drum pattern #1, page 12).

Exercise 1 Bass drum pattern (basic)

You can accent the pattern on beat 2, the low surdo note.

Exercise 2 Bass drum pattern accenting the second beat, the low surdo note

Adding the hi-hat on the upbeats (1 + 2 +) helps push the rhythm.

Exercise 3 Bass drum and hi-hat pattern (basic)—Slow to medium tempo

16

Here is the same exercise played at a faster tempo.

Exercise 4 Bass drum and hi-hat pattern (basic)—Faster tempo

HI-HAT VARIATIONS

The following hi-hat variations can be played with many of the different patterns shown in this book. These variations can add color and change a song very subtly. At first, try playing these hi-hat variations along with the same pattern, not only to hear the different textures but also as a good independence exercise.

Exercise 5 Hi-hat variations
Variation 1—Hi-hat on quarter-notes

Variation 2—Hi-hat on eighth-notes

Variation 3—Hi-hat opening on beat 2—The low surdo note

Variation 4—Hi-hat on up-beats

Now we will combine the snare and toms with the most common bass drum and hi-hat rhythm. Notice how the bass drum and hi-hat patterns fit with the snare drum and surdo parts—the rhythm should sound strong and full. Try to bring all the parts together to sound like a traditional samba ensemble.

Exercise 6 Batucada on full drumset with surdo parts and basic bass drum and hi-hat part

[Exercise 6a is the same as example 6, played at a faster tempo]

MORE SNARE DRUM PATTERNS FOR SAMBA

Let's look at other snare drum patterns that can be played with the basic bass drum and hi-hat patterns in the samba school style. The first pattern is often used in carnaval parades. The second sixteenth-note in the snare drum pattern is "buzzed," like a press roll. To buzz a note, reduce the natural rebound of the stick. The more pressure you apply, the tighter the buzz. Listen to the tape to help imitate the sound. The rhythm is called *maxixe*, which is a Brazilian dance influenced by the Cuban habanera, the polka and syncopated African rhythms. The sticking is RRLR, with the second right hand buzzed.

Exercise 1 Snare drum pattern #3—Maxixe

In the next example, all the sixteenth-notes are buzzed with accents on the downbeats and pick-up notes. The two unaccented notes are played lightly and are felt more than heard.

Exercise 2 Snare drum pattern #4 (Snare drum pattern #1 with buzzed notes)

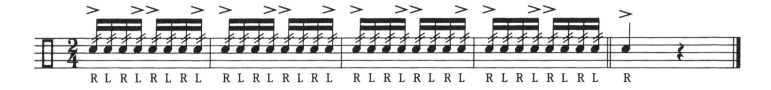

The next exercise alternates between normal strokes and buzzed notes.

Exercise 3 Four bars of snare drum pattern #1, to four bars of snare drum pattern #4

R L R L R L R L   R L R L R L R L   R L R L R L R L   R L R L R L R L

Simile

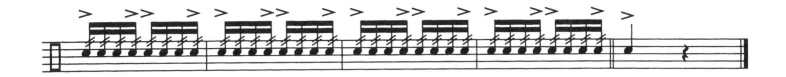

Now we can add buzzed notes to snare drum pattern #2, with an emphasis on the accented notes played with the right hand.

Exercise 4 Snare drum pattern #5 (Snare drum pattern #2 with buzzed notes)

R L R L R R L R   L R L R L R R L   R L R L R R L R   L R L R L R R L

R L R L R R L R   L R L R L R R L   R L R L R R L R   L R L R L R R L

Snare drum pattern #5 can also be accented on the snare drum rim:

Exercise 5 Snare drum pattern #5—Played on snare drum rim

Ⓡ = right rim shot

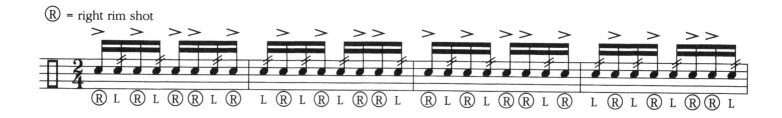

Now we will play the previous snare drum patterns with the basic bass drum and hi-hat pattern.

Exercise 6 Four previous snare drum patterns—With basic bass drum and hi-hat pattern

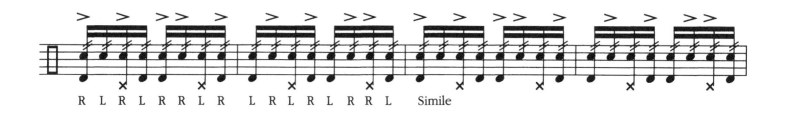

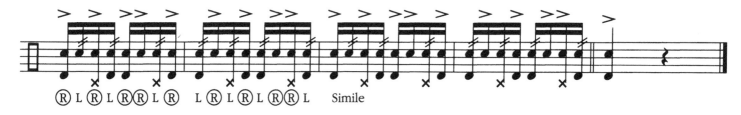

Here is a pattern that is played "reversed." We will begin with the snare drum, bass drum and hi-hat.

Exercise 1 Reverse pattern #1—Just snare drum part

R L L R L L R L   R L L R L R L L   R L L R L L R L   R L L R L R L R

R L L R L L R L   R L L R L R L R   R L L R L L R L   R L L R L R L R

Now we will add the middle surdo part played on middle tom.

Exercise 2 Reverse pattern #1—With snare drum and middle surdo (on middle tom)

The low surdo part can be added on the floor tom as follows:

Exercise 3 Reverse pattern #1—With snare drum, middle and low surdo parts

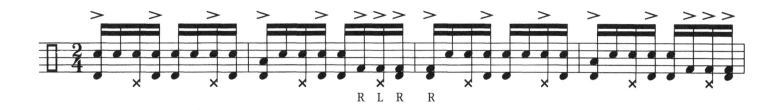

R L R   R

21

Finally, let's add the high surdo part on the small tom.

Exercise 4 Reverse pattern #1—With high, middle and low surdo parts

The following are some variations using different combinations of surdo parts:

Exercise 5 Reverse pattern #1—Variation 1—Double on middle tom

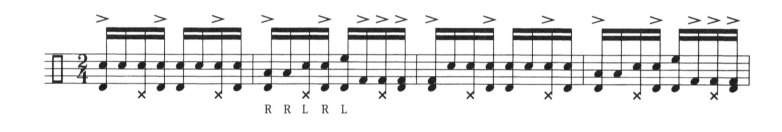

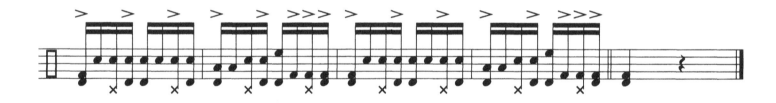

Exercise 6 Reverse pattern #1—Variation 2—Going down the toms

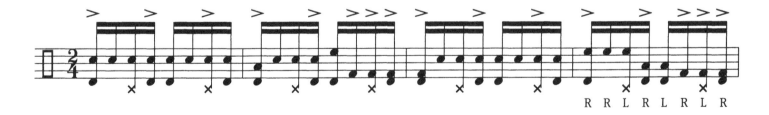

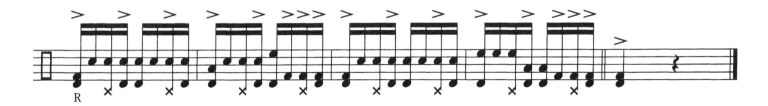

22

Exercise 7 Reverse pattern #1—Variation 3—Going up the toms

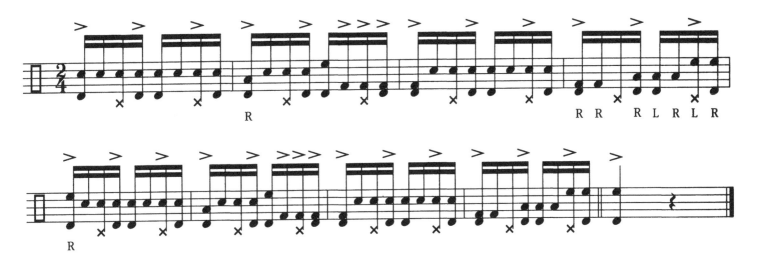

Exercise 8 Reverse pattern #1—Variation 4—mixing up the variations

Samba cruzado ("samba that crosses") refers to the particular sticking of this rhythm in which one hand crosses over the other. The right hand plays on the snare drum while the left hand plays on the toms.

Exercise 9 Samba cruzado—Basic pattern—With snare drum and surdo parts

You can add the floor tom to create this variation:

Exercise 10 Samba cruzado—With variation #1—On floor tom

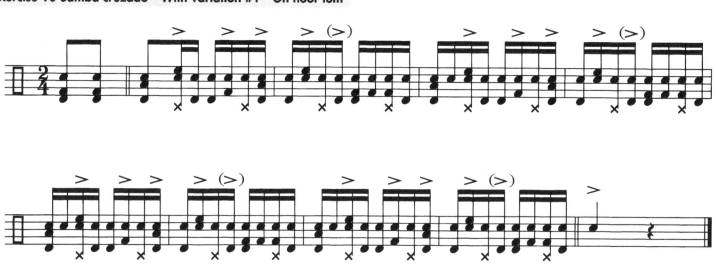

Now we will play constant eighth-notes on the hi-hat with the foot while opening the hi-hat with the stick in the second bar.

Exercise 11 Samba cruzado—Variation #2—WIth eighth-notes on hi-hat and hi-hat accent

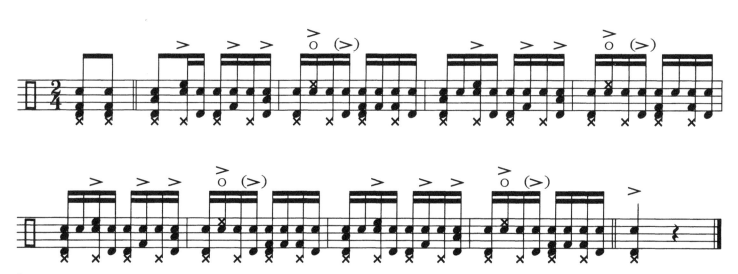

You can open the hi-hat on the low surdo note (beat 2) of each measure.

Exercise 12 Samba cruzado—Variation #3—With hi-hat open on the low surdo note

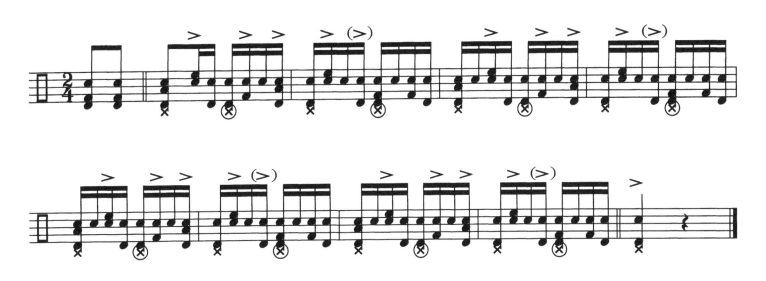

Try playing sixteenth-notes on the hi-hat instead of on the snare.

Exercise 13 Samba cruzado—Variation #4—With sixteenth-notes on hi-hat

Now we will play the same pattern substituting the snare for the small tom.

Exercise 14 Samba cruzado—Variation #5—Using the snare drum in the pattern

You can play the small tom instead of the middle tom or alternate between the two of them. Different surdo/tom combinations will produce different "melodies."

Exercise 15 Samba cruzado—Variation #6—Mixing up the figure on small and middle toms

Now try opening the hi-hat on the second sixteenth-note of each beat.

Exercise 16 Samba cruzado—Variation #7—WIth new hi-hat pattern

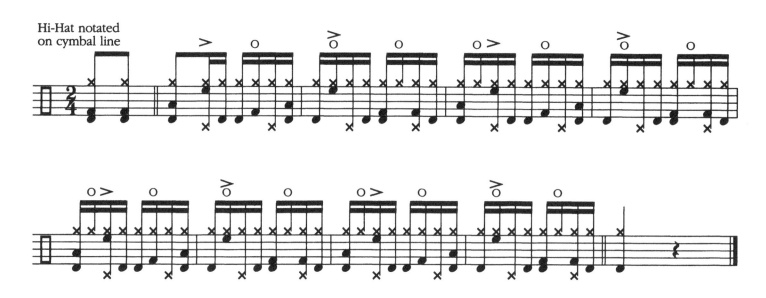

The next example is a combination of the two previous examples. The right hand plays sixteenth-notes on the cymbal and the left hand plays on the toms and hi-hat.

Exercise 17 Samba cruzado—Variation #8—WIth ride cymbal

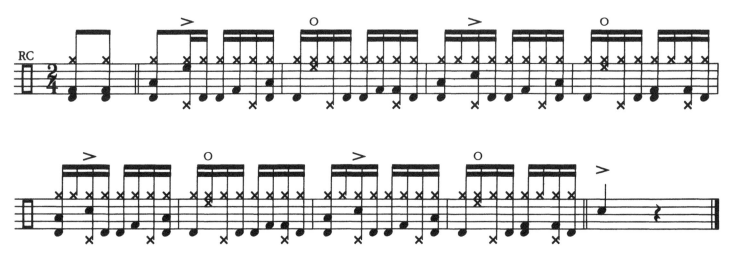

The next pattern was created by the great Brazilian drummer/percussionist Airto Moreira. Keep your heel down on the hi-hat pedal to help play the pattern.

Exercise 18 "Airto pattern"—Basic and with variations

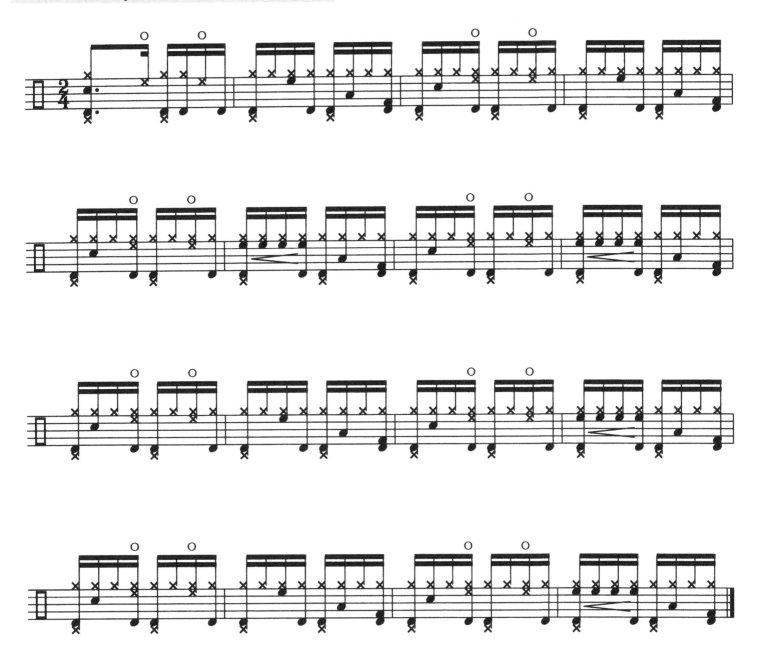

In most sambas, the pandeiro traditionally plays a constant sixteenth-note feel which gives a flowing *swing* to the rhythm. Let's hear the pandeiro play a simple pattern and listen to the unique phrasing of the sixteenth-notes.

Exercise 1 Pandeiro pattern [The second sixteenth-note is not turned as the audio cue says]

T=Thumb
F=Finger Tips
H=Heel

You can imitate the pandeiro rhythm on your hi-hat (straight sixteenths), as in the samba cruzado section. Or, you can open the hi-hat on the second sixteenth-note of each beat which is accented in the pandeiro and tamborim rhythms in samba. The hi-hat closes on the "and " of each beat.

Exercise 2 Hi-hat pattern #2—Playing the pandeiro figure

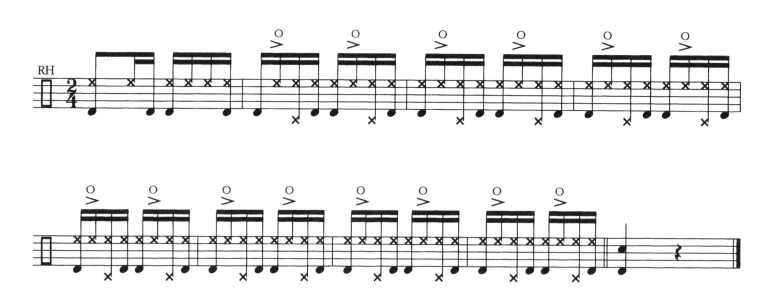

The tamborim pattern that we played on snare drum can also be played on the hi-hat. Notice how the cross-stick compliments the accents in the pattern.

Exercise 3 Hi-hat pattern #3—First four phrases hi-hat and bass drum—following four phrases with cross-stick added

28

This next pattern has a nice light feel with hi-hat accents in between the bass drum rhythm. We will play it first at a medium tempo, followed by a faster tempo. The sticking is RLRL.

Exercise 4 Hi-hat pattern #4—Medium tempo*   **Hi-hat pattern #4—Faster tempo**

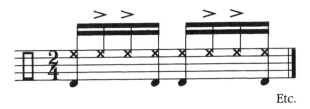

Etc.

SAMBA WITH HI-HAT PATTERNS

Our first ride cymbal pattern is three sixteenth-notes followed by a sixteenth-note rest. The fourth sixteenth-note can be played with a cross-stick or on the snare drum. You can also accent the bell of the ride cymbal on the last two sixteenth-notes of the pattern for an "upbeat" feel. When playing Brazilian rhythms, *lead* the groove with your right hand on the ride cymbal, rather than pushing the rhythm with your left hand on the snare drum.

Exercise 1 Ride cymbal pattern #1

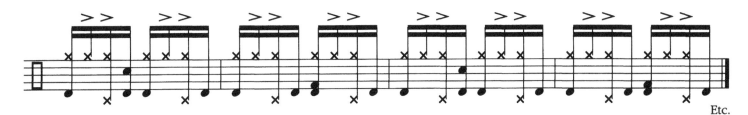

Etc.

You can play the tamborim pattern on your ride cymbal as we did earlier with the hi-hat and snare drum. As with the hi-hat pattern, notice how the cross-stick accents fit with the ride pattern.

Exercise 2 Ride cymbal pattern #2—Tamborim pattern on ride cymbal

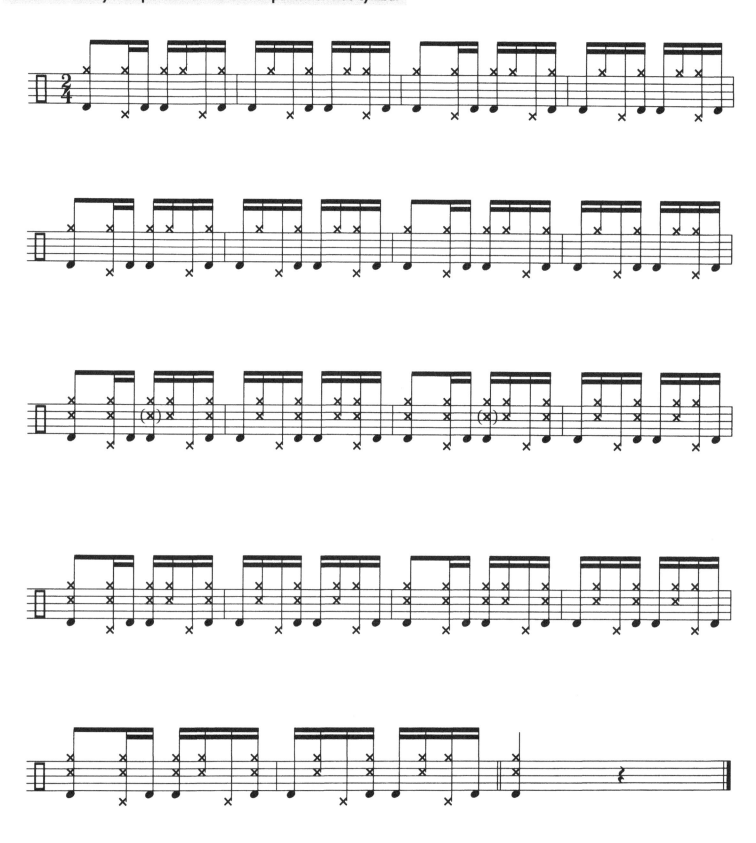

Once you become comfortable playing these basic feels on the ride cymbal, try working in the different cymbal patterns that you have learned.

Next is a great feel created by one of the most important innovators of Brazilian drumming, Edison Machado.

Exercise 3 Ride cymbal pattern #3—Edison Machado feel

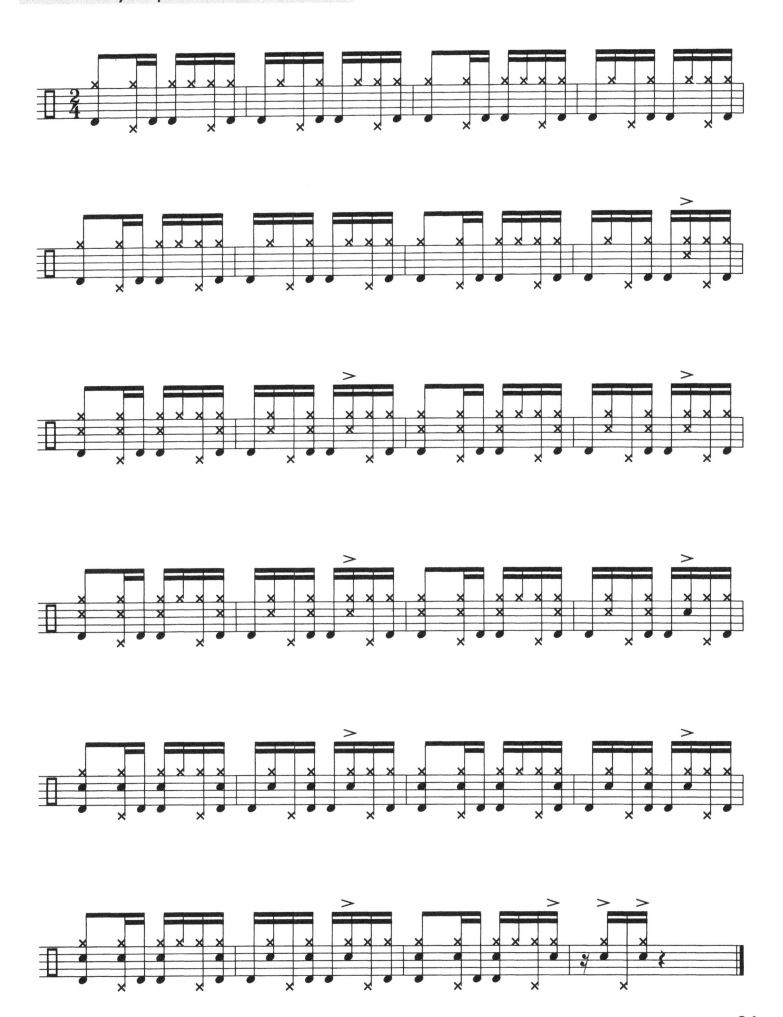

Playing Brazilian music with brushes can create different textures and feels. In the first pattern, the right hand plays sixteenth-notes and accents, while the left hand "swishes" on eighth-notes in small clockwise circles. The arrows indicate the direction of the brush strokes.

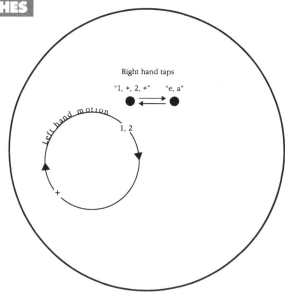

Exercise 1 Brush pattern #1

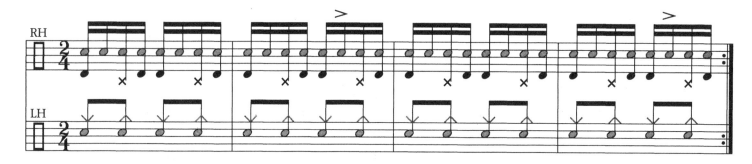

In this next pattern, the right hand plays the maxixe figure, swishing on the second sixteenth-note of each beat. The left hand circles under the right hand figure.

Exercise 2 Brush pattern #2

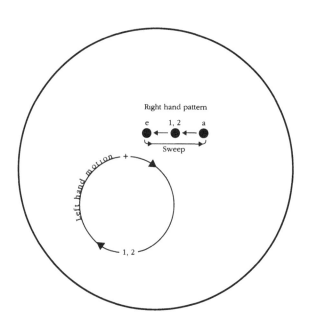

In this variation, the right hand plays an open hi-hat and snare drum accent on the second sixteenth-note of each beat with a sweeping "one handed flam" motion with the brush.

Exercise 2a Variation on brush pattern #2—Opening the hi-hat on the second sixteenth-note

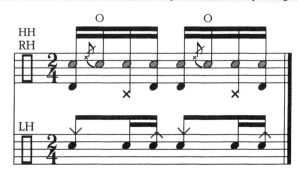

Here, the right hand plays three sixteenths and a rest (ride cymbal pattern #1), while the left hand accents the last sixteenth-note and circles the rest of the beat.

Exercise 3 Brush pattern #3

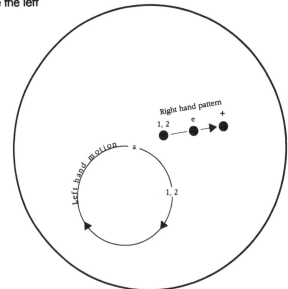

In the next pattern, the right hand plays accents while the left hand fills in the sixteenth-note pattern.

Exercise 4 Brush pattern #4

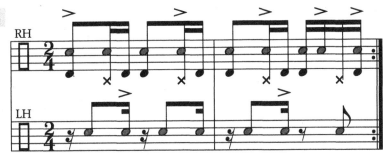

The following examples are different hi-hat variations that can be played with the previous brush pattern.

Exercise 4a Hi-hat variations that can be played with brush pattern #4

#1 Hi-hat on low surdo note

#2 Hi-hat on quarter-notes

#3 Hi-hat on eighth-notes

Now we will incorporate a bass drum variation that can be played with brush pattern 4. This bass drum pattern creates a completely different and syncopated feel.

Exercise 4b Bass drum variation that can be used with brush pattern #4

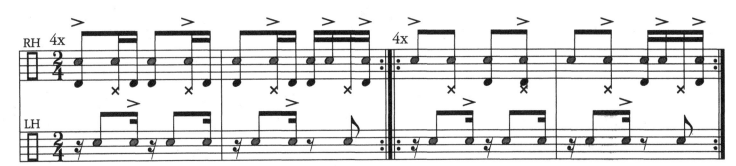

This next samba pattern can be played at medium or fast tempos.

Exercise 5 Samba with brush pattern #5—Played for medium and fast tempos

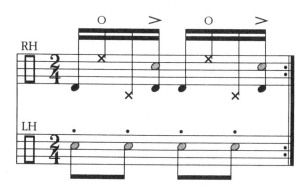

SAMBA WITH A FUNK FEEL

In this first pattern, we alternate *accents* on beat 2, with an anticipated accent on the last sixteenth-note of beat 1. Try playing these accents with a cross-stick, snare drum and floor tom.

Exercise 1 Playing on the snare drum rim, snare drum and snare drum and floor tom

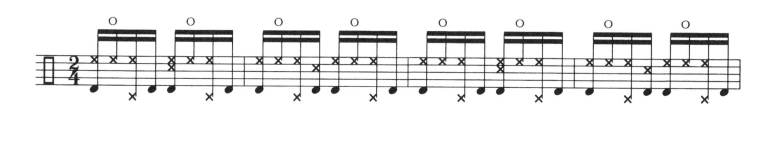

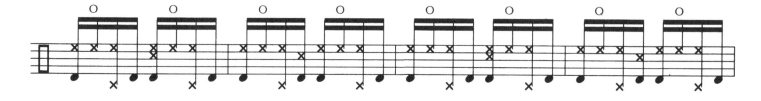

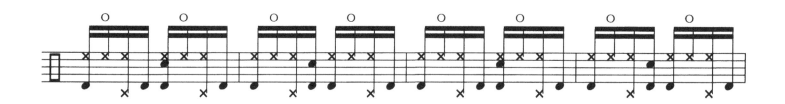

34

Here is a pattern using the anticipated accent on the last sixteenth-note of beat 1. Notice the constant eighth-notes in the hi-hat pattern.

Exercise 2 Samba funk feel pattern #2

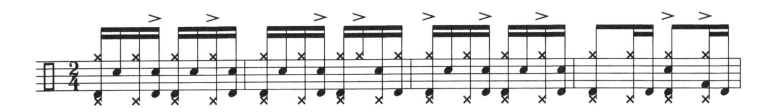

This pattern is a variation of pattern #2. The left hand plays the hi-hat (filling in the sixteenth-note pattern), while the right hand plays the ride cymbal and snare drum.

Exercise 2a Variation using hi-hat—With left hand on pattern #2

SAMBA DO PARTIDO ALTO

There are many different types and variations of samba. One of the most popular samba variations is ***samba do partido alto*** The *rhythm* of the samba do partido alto is often found in batucada. In the following example the partido alto rhythm is played by the ago-go bells and the tamborim pattern is played on the snare drum.

Exercise 1 Partido alto figure on ago-go bells—Over snare drum pattern #2

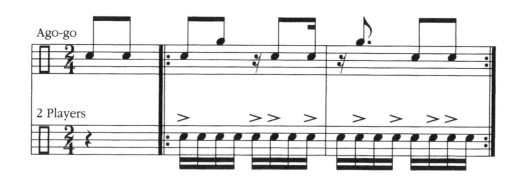

Partido alto is a two-bar pattern. One can start from the first or second measure of the pattern. The pick-up notes are optional.

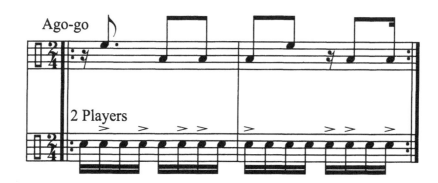

The partido alto rhythm functions as a polyrhythm against the "2" feel of samba and offers many possibilities on drumset. In this exercise we will play four bars of basic samba feel, followed by four bars of partido alto.

Exercise 2 Going from four bars of basic samba feel to four bars of basic partido alto feel

The next example is the same partido alto pattern using the snare drum instead of cross-stick.

Exercise 3 Basic partido alto figure with snare drum and bass drum

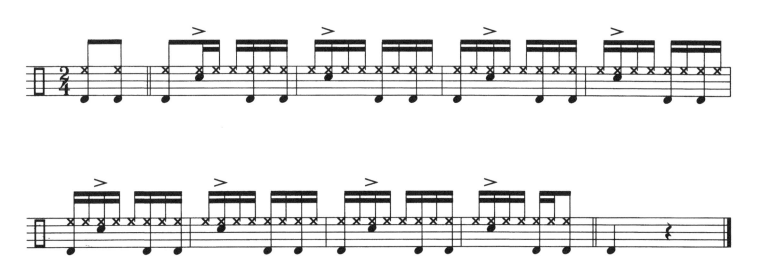

Now we will move the first snare drum accent from the "and" of beat 1 to the last sixteenth-note. Opening the hi-hat on the second sixteenth-note of each beat gives a subtle lift to the rhythm.

Exercise 4 Partido alto variation #1

Once you are comfortable with the basic pattern, open the hi-hat on the second sixteenth-note of each beat. Here is the same pattern with the open hi-hat notated throughout.

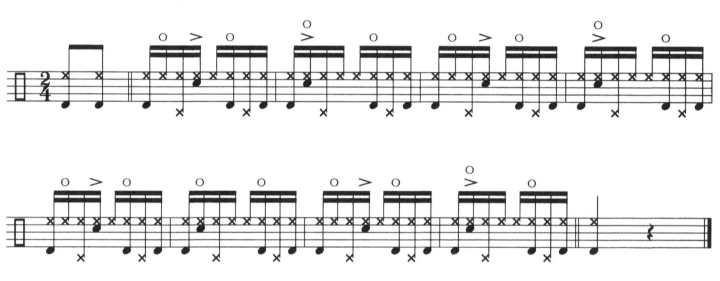

Now we will introduce a new hi-hat pattern and play four bars of basic partido alto feel, followed by four bars of variation #1.

Exercise 5 Four bars of basic partido alto figure to four bars of variation #1—With new hi-hat pattern

You can play the same pattern with sixteenth-notes on the hi-hat with the right hand (slow to medium tempos), or hand to hand for faster tempos.

Exercise 6 Four bars of basic partido alto figure to four bars of variation (#1)—With sixteenth-notes on the hi-hat

You can play the hi-hat and bass drum together while filling in the other notes on snare drum as follows:

Exercise 6a Four bars of basic partido alto figure to four bars of variation (#1)—Breaking up sixteenth-notes with the left hand on snare drum and right hand on hi-hat

R   R   R L R L L R L R   L R L L R L R L   R L R L L R L R   L R L L R L R L

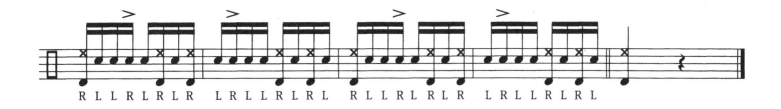

R L L R L R L R   L R L L R L R L   R L L R L R L R   L R L L R L R L

Here is a second variation:

Exercise 7 Partido alto—Variation #2—With two different bass drum patterns

R   R

Here is another variation with a different bass drum pattern.

Exercise 8 Partido alto—Variation #3

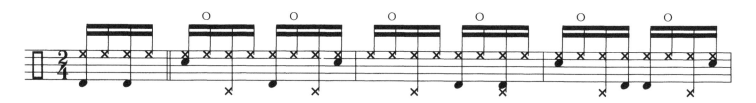

The following is a four-bar pattern combining different bass drum variations.

Exercise 9 Four-bar pattern mixing up the different bass drum patterns

Exercise 6 Four bars of basic partido alto figure to four bars of variation (#1)—With sixteenth-notes on the hi-hat

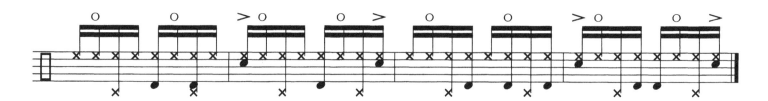

Here is a partido alto pattern from the great Brazilian percussionist Nana Vasconcelos.

Exercise 10 Partido alto pattern from Nana Vasconcelos

Here is another partido alto variation.

Exercise 11 Partido alto—Variation #4

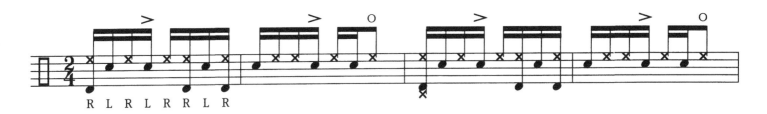

For more of a funk feel, partido alto can be played with quarter-notes on the hi-hat.

Exercise 12 Playing quarter-notes on the hi-hat with different partido alto variations

As with other styles of Brazilian music, the starting point of the pattern often depends on the phrasing of the melody. Another common way to start the partito alto pattern is with a snare drum hit leading into the bass drum phrase.

Related to the partido alto feel, you can play bass drum syncopations along with the hi-hat. We played these same bass drum accents in brush pattern #4b, which originated from variations played on the low surdo.

Exercise 13 Surdo variation on bass drum with hi-hat

You can also use the ride cymbal and snare drum with these bass drum accents. Accents on the cymbal can be played on the bell.

Exercise 13a Surdo variation on bass drum with ride cymbal and snare drum

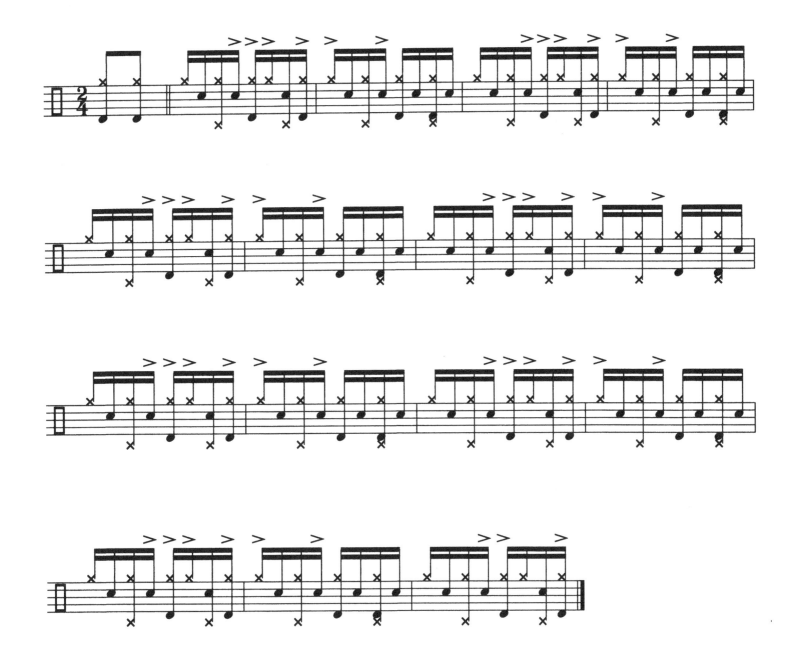

João Gilberto

In the late 1950's and early 60's, a group of young composers including Antonio Carlos Jobim, João Gilberto, Johnny Alf, João Donato, Carlos Lira, Marcos Valle, Dori Caymmi, Baden Powell and many others began to write and play in a new style called *bossa nova*.

Photo courtesy of Duduka Da Fonseca

BOSSA NOVA PATTERNS

The rhythm of the bossa nova is derived from samba. This first pattern is probably the best-known bossa nova pattern. The right hand plays on the hi-hat and the left hand plays a cross-stick pattern on the snare drum. The bass drum pattern is the same as in the samba patterns, but played at a slower tempo.

Exercise 1 Bossa nova pattern #1

Now we will reverse the measures. As in samba, the choice of which way to play the pattern is based on the phrasing of the melody.

Exercise 2 Bossa nova pattern #2

We can play the tamborim pattern that we used in snare drum pattern 2, with the cross-stick.
Note: You can also try this pattern reversed, by simply starting with the second measure.

Exercise 3 Bossa nova pattern #3—Tamborim figure on snare drum rim (cross-stick)

This bossa nova pattern features the partido alto rhythm (with cross-stick), and is often played in the accompanying guitar part.

Exercise 4 Bossa nova pattern #4—Emphasizing partido alto figure

One-bar phrases can also work well in the bossa nova style.

Exercise 5 One-bar phrases for bossa nova

Example #1

Antonio Carlos Jobim

Example #2

Example #3

This rhythm is also a one-bar pattern with a cross-stick on the last sixteenth-note of beat 1.

Exercise 6 Bossa nova pattern #5

As we saw in the samba section, the hi-hat can be opened on the second sixteenth-note of each beat.

Exercise 7 Hi-hat pattern #2—With first bossa nova pattern #1

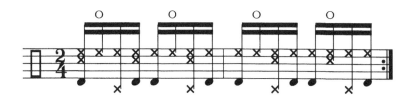

The hi-hat can be opened on beat 2 (low surdo note) along with a bass drum accent, as in the samba patterns.

Exercise 8 Opening the hi-hat on the low surdo note

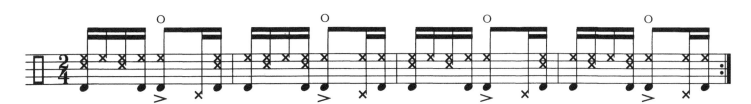

The hi-hat pattern can be played on the cymbal while playing up-beats on the hi-hat with your foot.

Exercise 9 Ride cymbal playing straight sixteenth-notes

Any of the bossa nova exercises that we played on hi-hat will also work on the ride cymbal. You can play the tamborim pattern on the ride cymbal and accent parts of the pattern on the snare drum (cross-stick) as follows:

Exercise 10 Tamborim pattern on ride cymbal

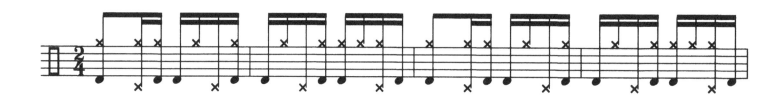

The brush patterns used for samba can also be used for bossa nova, especially the first three patterns from the Samba with Brushes section, page 32. We will play brush pattern #1 with different hi-hat variations. In this pattern, the right hand is playing constant eighth-notes with accents and the left hand circles on quarter-notes.

Exercise 11 Brush pattern #1

We can play the hi-hat on upbeats to add a bit of tension and forward motion to the rhythm.

Exercise 11a Brush pattern #1—With hi-hat variation on upbeats

Playing a "half-time" pulse can add a relaxed feeling to a ballad. As with brush pattern #1, the right hand plays eighth-notes and the left hand circles on quarter-notes.

Exercise 12 Half-time feel for bossa nova

A nice texture can be created by playing with a stick in one hand and a brush in the other. In the following example, the right hand plays the snare drum, hi-hat and ride cymbal with a brush, while the left hand plays on the snare drum (cross-stick).

Exercise 13 Patterns with brush in right hand and stick in left hand

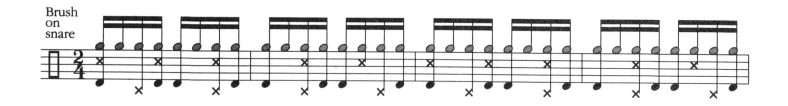

The following bossa nova brush example emphasizes beat 2, with a "china" cymbal.

Exercise 14 Playing the low surdo note on china cymbal or crash cymbal—With hi-hat on upbeats

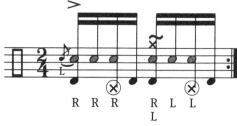

There is a lot of improvisation in playing bossa nova. You can choose any of the patterns that we have covered in this chapter and improvise around them, or change some of the patterns to fit a specific song or musical groove.

Luis Bonfá

Traditional baião group.

Photo courtesy of Edilberto Mendes

Baião (by-óh) is a popular type of music and dance from the northeast of Brazil. Baião is traditionally played on the *zabumba* drum (a wide, thin double headed drum), *triangle* and *accordion*. Other percussion instruments such as pandeiro, *caxixi* (small shakers), ago-go bells and snare drum are sometimes used. Here is a short example of baião played on these percussion instruments.

Traditional feel with percussion

Zabumba (o =open tone c=left hand dampening the head)

Triangle

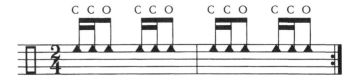

Snare drum

Ago-go bells

Pandeiro

We will begin with the basic bass drum and hi-hat pattern. The bass drum plays the rhythm played on the zabumba while the hi-hat plays the upbeats accented in the triangle pattern. The bass drum can also be played on the "and" of beat 2, as you will see in later exercises.

Exercise 1 Bass drum and hi-hat—Basic feel

Now we can add the snare drum. The snare drum is accented on the last sixteenth-note of beat 1 and the "and" of beat 2. The first snare drum accent plays at the same time as the second note of the bass drum pattern.

Exercise 2 Snare drum pattern #1—With bass drum and hi-hat

The sixteenth-notes on the snare drum can be "buzzed," as discussed in the samba section.

Exercise 3 Snare drum pattern #1—With buzzed notes

Now we will play the snare drum rhythm that was played in the traditional baião that we played at the beginning of this section. This is the maxixe feel that we saw in the samba section. The sticking that is presented (R RR L R), could also be played (R LL R L) or (R LL R R).

Exercise 4 Snare drum pattern #2

The first hi-hat example is based on the snare drum patterns we have been working on. Listen to how the accents with the hi-hat relate to the bass drum pattern—the first accent is *with* the bass drum and the second *answers* the bass drum.

In the next example the hi-hat is opened on the second, sixteenth-note of each beat, and closed on the following sixteenth-note, as in the samba section.

Exercise 1 Snare drum pattern #1—On hi-hat

Exercise 2 Hi-hat pattern #2

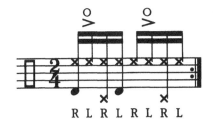

Here is a different sticking pattern that changes the phrasing of the rhythm. This sticking is based around the accents in the pattern and can help make the pattern more musical and less stiff.

Exercise 3 Hi-hat pattern #3

The following three examples are variations on hi-hat pattern #3:

Exercise 3a Hi-hat pattern #3 with variations

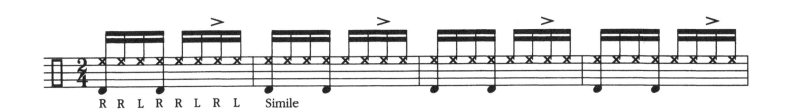

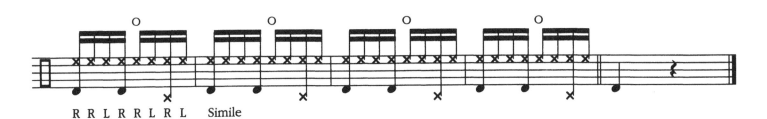

51

Here, the sticking represents the way the exercise was played on the tape. Two other options in the first bar could be (RLL RRLLRL) or (RLR LRLLR L).

Exercise 3b Hi-hat pattern #3—Another variation

R R R L R L L R L   R R L R R L R L

You can also play this pattern adding the snare drum or floor tom on the "and" of beat 2, and the middle tom on the last sixteenth-note of beat 1 as follows.

Exercise 3c Using the snare drum, floor tom and middle and floor tom—With variation

L L   L

To imitate the triangle played in traditional baião, play on the bell of the top hi-hat cymbal.

Exercise 4 Triangle part—On hi-hat bell

R L R L R L R L

The standard paradiddle sticking is (RLRR LRLL). If we change the order of the singles and doubles to (RLLR LLRL), the right hand will fall with the three-note bass drum pattern.

Exercise 1 Paradiddle on snare drum

Now we can break up the pattern between the snare drum and hi-hat. Use the same sticking and play the right hand on the hi-hat. If you like, you can play the original bass drum part without playing on the "and" of beat 2.

Exercise 2 Paradiddle broken between snare drum and hi-hat—With right hand playing hi-hat

Now we will break up the right hand between the hi-hat and snare drum.
For the following patterns you can try these different bass drum patterns:

Exercise 3 Broken paradiddle with right hand alternating between snare drum and hi-hat

53

Now we will add the toms to this paradiddle pattern.

Exercise 4 Broken paradiddle with different tom combinations

R L L R L L R L   R L L R L L R L   Simile

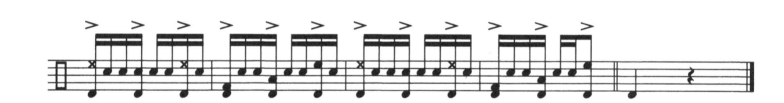

[There is not an Exercise 5, please go on to Exercise 6]

Now we will add the ride cymbal and different tom variations.

Exercise 6 Broken paradiddle with ride cymbal and variations on toms

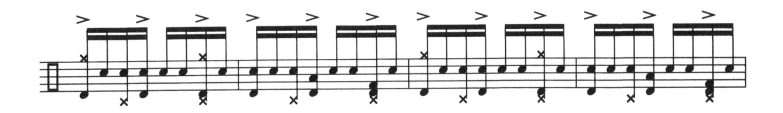

For the following pattern, play the left hand on the hi-hat instead of the snare drum.

Exercise 7 Broken paradiddle—Right hand plays ride cymbal—Left hand plays hi-hat

R L L R L L R L   R L L R L L R L

Try alternating between the ride cymbal and snare drum with your right hand as follows.

Exercise 8 Broken paradiddle—Right hand playing ride cymbal and snare drum—Left hand plays hi-hat

R L L R L L R L   R L L R L L R L

Now add the toms to the pattern.

Exercise 9 Variation on the previous exercise (#8)—Using toms

Playing the same pattern, open the hi-hat on the second sixteenth-note of each beat with the left hand.

Exercise 10 Broken paradiddle—Left hand plays hi-hat—Opening the hi-hat

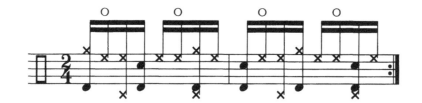

Now add the toms:

Exercise 11 Variation on the previous exercise (#10) using toms

Now try reversing the snare drum and hi-hat accents in the paradiddle.

Exercise 12 Broken paradiddle between snare drum and hi-hat—Reversing snare drum and hi-hat accents

R L L R L L R L   R L L R L L R L

You can experiment with this reverse sticking with all the previous patterns to create new combinations.

You can play other syncopations on the bass drum against the different hi-hat or snare drum patterns. These bass drum variations are traditionally played on the zabumba.

Exercise 1 Bass drum variations with hi-hat

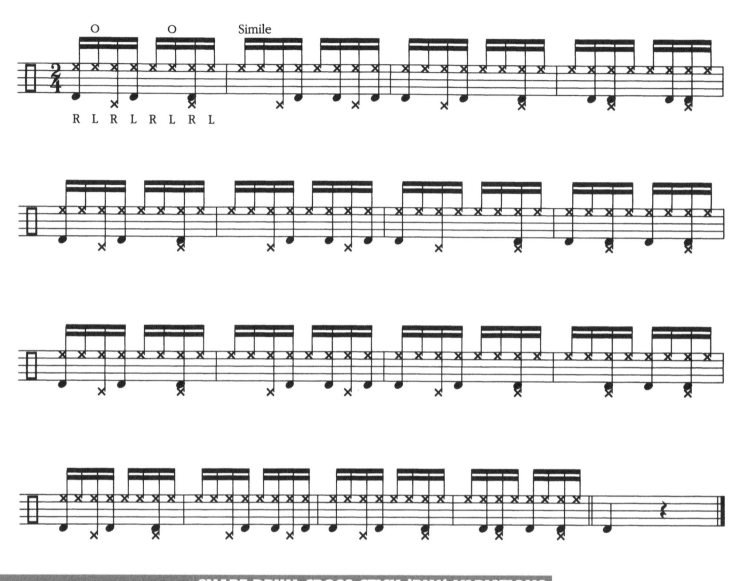

SNARE DRUM CROSS-STICK (RIM) VARIATIONS

Playing cross-stick patterns on the snare drum is very popular when playing baião patterns. Several variations can be played. We will begin by playing quarter-notes.

Exercise 1 Playing quarter-notes on the rim

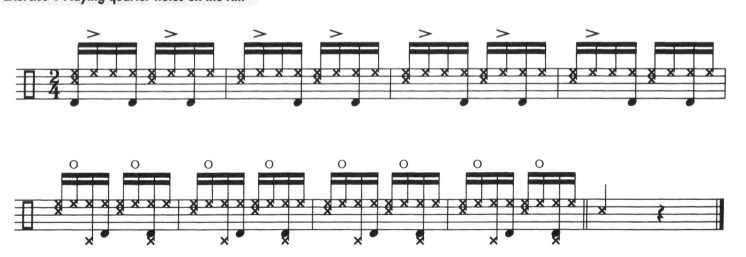

You can answer the bass drum pattern by playing a cross-stick on the "and" of beat 2.

Exercise 2 Playing the rim on beat 4 ("and" of beat 2, counting in sixteenth-notes)

Playing a cross-stick on beat 2, creates a backbeat feel.

Exercise 3 Playing the snare drum rim on "3" (written in 2/4—cross-stick on beat 2)

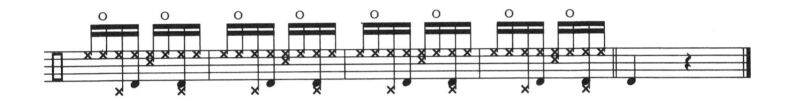

BAIÃO—RIDE CYMBAL PATTERNS

The first ride cymbal pattern consists of three sixteenth-notes followed by a sixteenth-note rest. This pattern has a strong downbeat feel with a cross-stick on each beat.

Exercise 1 Ride cymbal pattern #1

As a variation to the bass drum pattern in Exercise 1, the bass drum can be played on the second sixteenth-note of beat 2, replacing the "and" of beat 2.

Exercise 1a Ride cymbal pattern #1—With bass drum syncopation

The next pattern has snare drum cross-sticks on the upbeats.

Exercise 2 Ride cymbal pattern #2

The next sticking pattern (RRLR RLRL) is split between the cymbal and cross-stick, and the bell of the cymbal and snare drum.

Exercise 3 Ride cymbal pattern #3

Here is a variation on the previous sticking pattern, incorporating the snare drum and toms.

Exercise 3a Ride cymbal pattern #3 — With toms

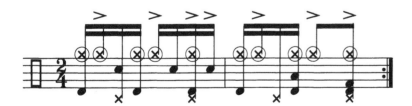

More variations with toms:

Exercise 3b Variations on ride cymbal pattern #3—With toms

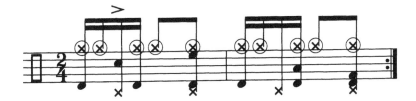

Exercise 3c Another variation on ride cymbal pattern #3—With toms

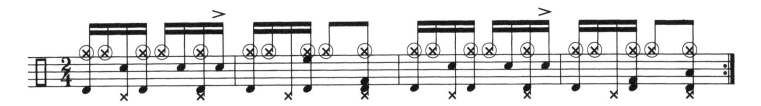

Again, once you become familiar with these patterns, you can mix them together or use them as a starting point from which to improvise.

Luis Gonzaga "The King of Baião"

This first pattern has an accent or "backbeat" played with a cross-stick, snare, and floor tom, with upbeats on hi-hat and ride cymbal. The bass drum rhythm is the three-note baião pattern.

Exercise 1 Upbeats on hi-hat and ride cymbal*

The broken paradiddle figure that we played earlier can be adapted to a baião funk feel by playing the right hand on hi-hat or cymbal, and the left hand on the snare drum with an accent in the second bar on beat 2.

Exercise 2 Broken paradiddle between hi-hat and snare drum, and ride cymbal and snare drum

R L L R L L R L   R L L R L L R L   Simile

62

This next pattern uses "hand to hand" sticking with the right hand playing eighth-notes on the hi-hat and an accent on beat 2 in the second bar of the pattern.

Exercise 3 Variations on exercise 2—Using upbeats on hi-hat*

L R L   L R L   L R   L L R L

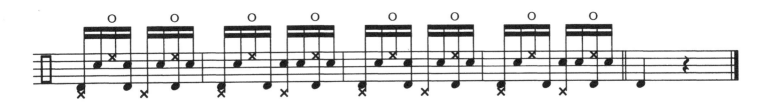

63

Here is a pattern that we played earlier in the baião section, adapted to a funk feel.

Exercise 4 Hi-hat pattern #3a—On hi-hat and ride cymbal

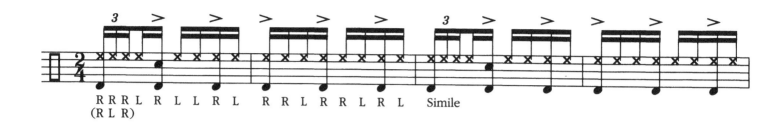

R R R L R L L R L R R L R R L R L Simile
(R L R)

R R R L R L L R L R R L R R L R L Simile
(R L R)

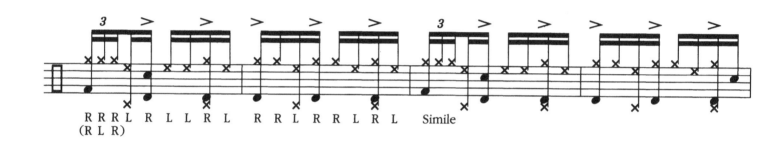

R R R L R L L R L R R L R R L R L Simile
(R L R)

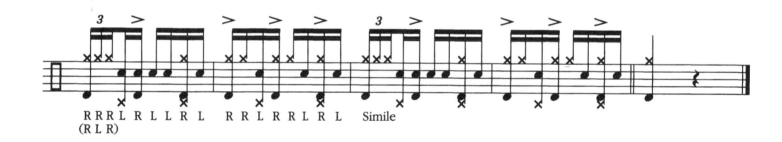

R R R L R L L R L R R L R R L R L Simile
(R L R)

Afoxe (a-foo-sháy) is a rhythm and dance from Bahia, a northeastern state in Brazil which has a large West African population. Afoxe is from the ritual music of Candomble, which is a Yoruba (Nigerian) religion in Brazil. Traditionally played on percussion, here is a pattern that can be played on drumset.

Exercise 1 Variation using hi-hat and ride cymbal

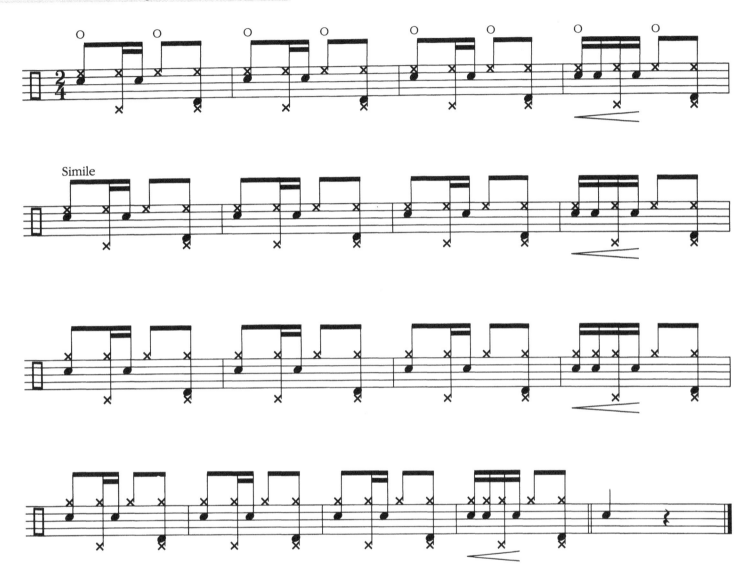

Now the same pattern with a different bass drum part:

Exercise 2 Variation using hi-hat

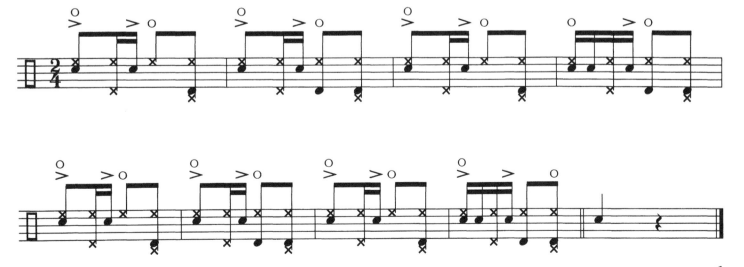

Caterete (ca-teh-de-tay) is a rhythm and dance with roots in the Indian culture of Brazil.

Exercise 1 Caterete—Basic pattern using hi-hat and snare drum rim

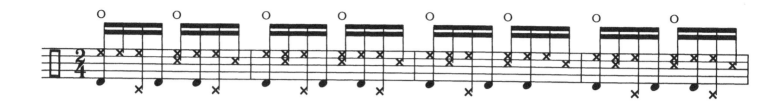

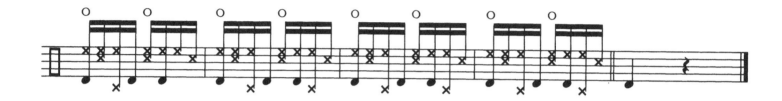

Now play the cross-stick rhythm on the snare drum.

Exercise 2 Caterete—Basic pattern using hi-hat and snare drum

We can play the hi-hat pattern on the ride cymbal and cymbal bell.

Exercise 3 Caterete—Basic pattern and variation using ride cymbal and ride cymbal bell

Afro-Brazilian Orchestra

Photo courtesy of Edilberto Mendes

Maracatu (ma-ra-ca-tóo) is a processional dance which takes place in the city of Recife in the northeast state of Pernambuco. The music which accompanies this dance is thought to have its roots in the ceremonies in which African kings were coronated.

Here is an example of maracatu played in a folkloric style.

To help find beat 1 of the maracatu pattern, listen for the phrase played on the zabumba, or follow the melody of the ago-go bells.

Maracatu—Folkloric feel

Zabumba

Snare drum

Triangle

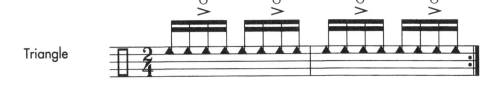

Ago-go bells

Caxixi

67

On drumset, you can play the syncopations of the zabumba on the toms.

Exercise 1 Maracatu on drumset—Slow to medium feel

When playing faster tempos, the sticking changes and a simpler pattern is played with the bass drum.

Exercise 2 Maracatu pattern for drumset for faster tempos—Played first at slower tempo—Followed by faster tempo

Here is a tom variation of the same pattern.

Exercise 2a Maracatu pattern for faster tempos—With variations on toms

68

Marcha (mársh-a), which borrowed rhythms from military parades, became a popular dance for carnaval festivities in Brazil. Here is the basic feel. The roll at the end of the pattern can be played as a loose press roll with both hands, as on the tape, or as a 9 or 13-stroke roll, depending on the tempo.

Exercise 1 Marcha—Basic feel

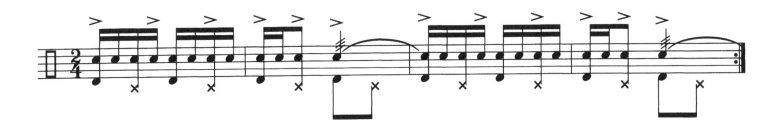

Derived from marcha, *frevo* (fráy-vo) is an instrumental dance from Recife, in the northeast state of Pernambuco. Popular during carnaval time, frevo is generally played at a fast tempo with a syncopated "2" feel.

Exercise 2 Frevo—Basic feel

You can play a syncopated pattern with your bass drum underneath the snare drum pattern as follows:

Exercise 3 Frevo with bass drum syncopations

Many of the rhythms that we have covered can be played in different time signatures.

Although it may seem surprising due to its strong "2" feel, samba rhythms fall quite naturally into 3/4 time. The following samba example in 3/4 is in three sections:

A Snare/bass/hi-hat. The snare drum pattern falls naturally into the time signature along with the bass drum and hi-hat playing the basic samba pattern.

B Adding the toms. This pattern shows how the surdo parts can be played on the toms in 3/4. The low surdo note is still played on beat 2, but with the pattern resolving from beat 3, to beat 1.

C Ride cymbal. This pattern shows how you can open up on the ride cymbal and toms.

Exercise 1 Samba in 3/4 time

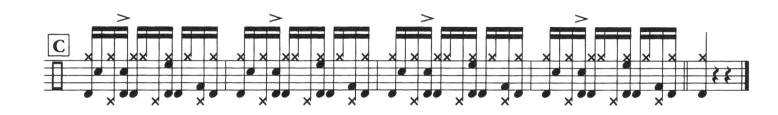

Samba can work well in 7/8 meter as well. You can think of this pattern as dropping an eighth-note from the second bar of the normal 2/4 samba rhythm.

Exercise 2 Samba in 7/8 time

Partido alto patterns can work in 7/8 time. The hi-hat opens on beat 7 and closes on beat 1.

Exercise 3 Partido alto in 7/8

Here is a more syncopated version with added bass drum notes:

Exercise 3a Partido alto in 7/8—First variation

Duduka Da Fonseca and Carlinhos "Pandeiro De Ouro" (Golden Tambourine)   Photo courtesy of Duduka Da Fonseca

To conclude, we would like to demonstrate, with Trio da Paz, how some of the ideas and patterns in this book can be used. On the **recording**, you will hear a medium-tempo samba followed by an uptempo samba. The musicians are as follows:

"Trio da Paz"

Romero Lubambo   *Guitar and guitar synthesizers*
Nilson Matta   *Acoustic bass*
Duduka Da Fonseca   *Drums*

We hope that this has been a valuable and enjoyable learning experience for you. Recordings and live performances of Brazilian music will help you discover how these rhythms can be used in a variety of musical situations. The discography that follows will help you in your search. For more information on Brazilian music and where to find books, videos and resource centers, see the bibliography.

Duduka Da Fonseca and Bob Weiner

GLOSSARY

DISCOGRAPHY

BIBLIOGRAPHY

AFOXE   (a-foo-sháy)   A rhythm and dance from Bahia, a state in northeast Brazil which has a large West African population from Nigeria. Afoxe comes from the ritual music of Candomble, the Yoruba (Nigerian) religion in Brazil.

AGO-GO BELLS   (a-go-gó)   West African in origin, ago-go bells consist of three different sized metal bells welded together that are often used to play the rhythms of baião and maracatu. In the 1950's ago-go bells were introduced into the Escola De Samba.

BAHIA   (by-eé-ah)   A state in the northeast of Brazil with a large West African population.

BAIÃO   (by-óh)   A popular music and dance from the northeast of Brazil, traditionally played with zabumba drum, triangle, and accordion.

BATUCADA   (ba-too-cá-da)   Batucada refers to samba played only on percussion instruments.

BERIMBAU   (beh-rim-bów)   A musical bow made of wood with a metal string and gourd attached for resonance. Used to accompany the dance/martial art form capoeira.

BOSSA NOVA   A Brazilian-born musical style of the late 50's and early 60's that combined sophisticated melodies, lyrics and European-influenced harmony with a subtle, samba-based rhythm. Important bossa nova composers and originators include João Gilberto, Antonio Carlos Jobim, Johnny Alf, João Donato and Eumir Deodato.

CAIXA   (káh-sha)   A thin snare drum played in samba schools. The caixa is sometimes called *tarol*.

CAPOIERA   (cup-oo-éh-rah)   A folkloric dance and martial art form played to music.

CANDOMBLE   (con-dom-bláy)   A West African (Yoruba) religion practiced in Bahia.

CATERETE   (ca-téh-de-tay)   A rhythm and dance with roots in the Indian (Native American) culture of Brazil.

CHORO OR CHORINHO
    sho-ro, sho-reen-yo   An instrumental music which evolved out of the tangos, polkas and waltzes played by Brazilian dance band musicians at the turn of the century. Over the years, while the European harmonic and melodic elements remained, these earlier rhythms were slowly replaced by variations of samba.

CUICA   (gwée-ka)   A single headed drum with a rod connected to the underside of the drum head. The rod is pulled with a wet cloth which produces friction and creates the sound of the instrument.

ESCOLA DE SAMBA   (samba school)   A large group that can range in size from 3,000 to 7,000 singers and dancers (including as many as 500 percussionists) that rehearses throughout the year in preparation for competition in the annual carnaval celebrations

FREVO   (fráy-vo)   A dance and rhythm derived from marcha. Frevo originated in Recife, in the Northeast state of Pernambuco, and is usually danced during carnaval.

GANZA   (gáhn-za)   A cylindrical metal instrument filled with stones or pieces of metal that is shaken back and forth.

MAXIXE   (ma-sháy-shay)   A Brazilian dance influenced by the Cuban habanera, the polka and syncopated African rhythms.

MARACATU   (ma-ra-ca-tóo)   A processional dance which takes place in the city of Recife in the Northeast state of Pernambuco. It is believed to have its origins in the ceremonies in which African kings were coronated.

MARCHA   (mársh-a)   A popular dance for carnaval which uses rhythms from military parades.

PANDEIRO (pahn-dáy-roh) The pandeiro, a tambourine with jingles, is very popular in many different types of Brazilian music. The playing of the pandeiro requires a great deal of skill and technique.

PARTIDO ALTO (par-tée-do ál-to) A popular samba style whose distinct rhythm has become a style of its own.

REPINIQUE (or REPIQUE)
(heh-pah-née-kee or heh-pée-kee) A double-headed drum carried over the shoulder and played with one or two sticks, or with your hands, that acts as a "calling" instrument signalling cues to the other players. Introduced into the Escola De Samba in the 1950's, it's sound can be recognized as being similar to that of a high timbale.

SAMBA (sáhm-ba) Brazil's most popular national musical style with both African and Portuguese influences.

SAMBA CRUZADO (sáhm-ba cru-sá-doh) "Samba that crosses," referring to this particular sticking pattern in which one hand crosses over the other to play the rhythm.

SURDO (sóor-doe) Surdos are different sized, low-pitched drums commonly used in samba schools. The rhythmic pulse of the surdos creates the heartbeat of samba.

TAMBORIM (tam-bo-réem) A single-headed drum, smaller than a tambourine and without jingles. The tamborim is held with one hand and played with a stick in the other hand.

WHISTLES In the Escola De Samba, whistles are used by the director to signal previously established cues, including entrances, cut-offs and dynamic changes, to the ensemble.

AFRO-BRAZILIAN SACRED AND FOLKLORIC MUSIC

Afro-Brazilian Religious Music, Lyrichord LLST 7135 (LP) Ritual music of Candomble, the West African (Yoruba) religion practiced in Salvador, Bahia.

Amazonia–Cult Music of Brazil, Lyrichord LLCT 7300 Afro-Brazilian religious music.

Black Music of South America—In Praise of Oxala and Other Gods, Nonesuch H-72036 Black music of Colombia, Ecuador and Brazil.

Afros e Afoxes da Bahia, Mango 539.839-4 Contemporary folk music from black musicians in Bahia.

Viva Brasilia, Accord (Time Plus) 330 762 (CD) MU 767 Includes the maracatu rhythm .

Brazil: Forro—Music For Maids and Taxi Drivers, Rounder C-5044 A cajun-like folk music of the northeast, using vocals, accordion and percussion.

Mendes, Sergio and Brazil '77, *Primal Roots,* A&M Records SP-4353.

SAMBA (BATUCADA, CARNAVAL AND FOLK STYLES)

Alma Brasileira–Mocidade Independente Padre Miguel, Warner Bros. (Brazil) 88.007

Bateria Nota, Top Tape TT 061 (cassette). Top Tape puts out many tapes of batucada. Top Tape Musica Ltda., Rua Alice 97, Laranjerias, Rio de Janeiro, Brazil (Phone 265-5820)

Batucada Fantastica–Volume 3, Luciano Perrone e Seus Ritmistas Brasileiros. Musidisc (Hara International) K7-017. Very innovative use of percussion, voice and drumset.

Batucada #4 (Os Reis do Batuque) A Magica e a Empolgacao dos Ritmos do Brasil (The Explosion of the Exciting Brazilian Rhythms), Philips 7128-205 Batucada as well as examples of partido alto, baião, frevo, maracatu and other Brazilian rhythms.

Sambas de Enredo, Carnaval '89 Gravacoes originais: Das Escolas de Samba do Grupo 1A, RCA Kaiser (LP) 122.00002 & MC 772.00002 An excellent compilation of the top samba schools and their competing songs for each year of carnaval.

Brazil Roots: Samba, Rounder CD 5045 Field recordings of folk-style samba.

O Samba (Samba and Pagode), Brazil Classics 2 Warner Bros. 26019.2 (CD) A great collection of popular samba singers and recordings compiled by David Byrne.

CONTEMPORARY SINGERS

Ben, Jorge, *Tropical,* Island ILPS 9390

Buarque, Chico, *Chico Buarque,* Barclay 825-161-1 (LP) 825-161-4 (cassette)

Buarque, Chico, *Almanaque,* Ariola 201640 (LP) 401640 (cassette)

Bosco, Joao, *Banda Lhismo,* RCA 110.0022
Bosco, Joao, *Comissao de Frente,* Ariola 201.905 (Lp) 401.905 (Cassette)

Carvalho, Beth, *Traco de Uniao,* RCA 103.0560
Carvalho, Beth, *Beth,* RCA 7180027

Costa, Gal, *Cantar,* Philips 6349.117
Costa, Gal, *Fantasia,* Philips 6328.365

Djavan, *Alumbramento,* EMI 064.422859
Djavan, *Seduzir,* EMI 31C-06442288D

Villa, Martinho da, *Canta Canta, Minha Gente* RCA Victor 110.0002
Villa, Martinho da, *Maravilha de Cenario* RCA Victor 110.0008

Gil, Gilberto, *Ficha Tecnica,* Philips 6349.034
Gil, Gilberto, *Realce,* Elektra BR 32.038

Lins, Ivan, *Ivan Lins, A Noite,* EMI 064-422849
Lins, Ivan, *Daquilo que eu sei,* Philips 6328-341

Joyce, *Ao Vivo,* EMI 364.793227-2

Nascimento, Milton, *Miltons,* Columbia CK 45239-2
Nascimento, Milton, *Clube da Esquina,* EMI 664.791606-2
Nascimento, Milton, *A Barca dos Amantes (Ship of Lovers),* Verve 831349-2 wth special guest Wayne Shorter.

Regina, Elis, *Elis, Essa Mulher,* Warner Bros. BR 36.113
Regina, Elis, *Elis e Tom,* Philips 6349.112
Regina, Elis, *Elis Regina–Montreux Jazz Festival,* Elektra BR 22.032-A

BOSSA NOVA

Gilberto, João, *João Gilberto,* Polydor 2451-037
Gilberto, João, *The Legendary João Gilberto—The Original Bossa Nova Recordings (1958-1961),* World Pacific B4-93891 (cassette). Includes the groundbreaking "Chega de Saudade" recording.

Gilberto, Astrud, *Astrud Gilberto and the James Last Orchestra,* Polygram Jazz 422-831-123-2 (with Duduka Da Fonseca)

Jobim, Antonio Carlos, *Passarim,* Verve 4228 332341
Jobim, Antonio Carlos, *Stone Flower,* Epic/Associated ZK45480
Jobim, Antonio Carlos, *Tide,* A&M Records SP 3031

BAIÃO

Gonzaga, Luis, *O Rei Volta Pra Casa,* RCA 710.0568

Dominguinhos, *Apos tu Certo,* Fontana 6470.617
Dominguinhos, *Domingo Enino,* Philips 6349.178

CHOROS (CHORINHOS)

Reis, Dilermando, Azevedo, Waldir *Os Grandes Solistas Volume 4,* Seta, 1-10-405-017 (LP), 1-10-702-017 (cassette)

Bandolim, Jacob do, *Valsas Brasileiras*, RCA Camden 107.0323

Bandolim, Jacob do, *Ao Mestre Jacob do Bandolim com Saudade*, RCA Camden 107.0201

Mooro, Paulo, *Mistura e Manda*, Braziliod BRCD 4012

Pixinguinha, *Pixinguinha e Benedito Lacerda –Choros Imortais*, AMC records AMCLP 5128

BRAZILIAN JAZZ AND PROGRESSIVE MUSIC

Banana, Milton, *Aos Amigos Tom, Chico e Vinicius*, RCA CD-10030

Brackeen, JoAnne, *Breath of Brazil*, featuring Eddie Gomez and and Duduka Da Fonseca, Concord Picante   CCD-4479

Caymmi, Dori, *Brasilian Serenata*, Q West 9265732

Gismonti, Egberto, *Sanfona*, ECM 1203-04, 829391-2

Gismonti, Egberto, *No Caipira*, EMI-Odeon 064-422836

Horta, Toninho, *Diamond Land*, Verve Forecast 835183-2

Mann, Herbie, *Jasil Brazz*, RBI, RBIC1401 (with Duduka Da Fonseca)

Mendes, Sergio, *The Beat of Brazil*, Atlantic Records SD-1480

Milito, Helcio, *Kilombo*, Antilles New Directions 7-90629-2

Moreira, Airto, *The Essential Airto featuring Flora Purim and Special Friends*, Buddah Records BDS 5668-2

Moreira, Airto and Flora Purim, *The Colours of Life*, In and Out Records CD001

Pascoal, Hermeto, *Lagoa da Canoa Municipio de Arapiraca*, Sigla 7714 DK-R, DK 018

Pascoal, Hermeto, *So Nao Toca Quem Nao Quer*, Verabra Records 19

Roditi, Claudio, *Two of Swords*, Candid Records (with Duduka Da Fonseca)

Romao, Dom Um, *Hotmosphere*, Pablo 2310-777

Salvador, Dom, *Minha Familia*, Muse Records MR 5085

The Zimbo Trio, *The Zimbo Trio*, Liberty Records Pacific Jazz ST-20103 (LP), PJ-10103 (cassette)

Tamba 4, *We and the Sea*, A&M (CTI) A&M-SP 3004

Vasconcelos, Nana, *Saudades*, ECM 1147 829380-2

Mulligan, Gerry, with Jane Duboc, *Paraiso*, Telarc CD83361 (with Duduka Da Fonseca)

Trio Da Paz, *Brasil From the Inside*, Concord Picante, CCD-4524

Brackeen, Joanne, *Breath of Brazil*, Concord Picante, CCD-4479

Gilberto, Astrud, *Astrud Gilberto Plus James Last Orchestra*, Polygram

Gilberto, Astrud, *Temperance*, Canyon International

Gilberto, Astrud, *Live in New York*, Canyon International

Brazilian Nights Featuring Romero Lumambo, *Rio Wave*, Q Records

AS A LEADER
Duduka Da Fonseca, *Samba Jazz Fantasia*, Malandro Records 71018

AS A CO-LEADER
Trio da Paz, *Brasil From The Inside*, Concorde Picante, ccd 4524

Trio da Paz, *Black Orpheus*, KOKO 1299

Trio da Paz, *Partido Out*, Malandro Records 71005

Trio da Paz, *Café*, Malandro Records

Dom Salvador, Rogerio Botter Maio, Duduka Da Fonseca, *Transition*, Bomba Records, Japan, 22067

Phil Woods, *Astor & Elis*, Chesky, JD 146

John Scofield, *Quiet*, Verve, POCJ 1343

Tom Harrel, *The Art of Rhythm*, RCA Victor, 09026-68924-2

Claudio Roditi, *Samba Manhattan Style*, Reservoir, CD 139

Slide Hampton, *Slide Plays Jobim*, Alleycat, 20021

Antonio Carlos Jobim, *Antonio Brasileiro*, Globo Columbia, 419.058

Lee Konitz & The Brazilian Band, *Brazilian Serenate*, TKCV 35028, Venus Records

Nancy Wilson, *A Nancy Wilson Christmas*, MCGJ 1008

Harry Allen, *Once Upon a Summertime*, BICJ, 31012(74321-672N-2)

Helio Alves, *Trios*, RSD cd 156

Toshiko Akiyoshi With Brazilian Friends, *Yes I Have No 4 Beat Today*, CRCJ 9132

Renee Rosnes, *Life on Earth*, Blue Note Records

Maucha Adnet, *Songs I Learned From Jobim*, Venus Records, TKCV 35023

Claudio Roditi, *Double Standards*, RSR cd 148

JoAnne Brackeen, *Take a Chance*, Concorde Picante, ccd 4502

Kenny Barron featuring Trio da Paz, *Canta Brazil*, Sunnyside Records (USA)/Universal (Europe)

Nilson Matta & Hendrik Meurkens, *Encontros*, Malandro, 71015

John Patitucci, *Communion*, Concord Jazz, ccd 4970-2

BOOKS, FILM, VIDEO, AND RESOURCE CENTERS COMPILED BY JOHN GRAY © 1989

AFRICA

Chernoff, John, *African Rhythm and African Sensibility,* Chicago: University of Chicago Press, 1979. 261 p. A leading work on African traditional drumming.

Graham, Ronnie, *The Da Capo Guide to Contemporary African Music.* New York: Da Capo Press, 1988. 315 p. A comprehensive discographical and geographical survey of contemporary African pop music styles.

LATIN AMERICAN AND THE CARIBBEAN
Books and Articles
Behague, Gerard and Robert Stevenson, *Latin America III: Afro-American Music,* from The New Grove Dictionary of Music and Musicians, Vol. 10, pp. 522–534.

Bergman, Billy, et. al., *Hot Sauces: Latin and Caribbean Pop.* New York: Quill, 1985. 144 p. Includes chapters on reggae, soca, New Orleans rhythm and blues, Haitian rara, salsa, Latin jazz and Brazilian pop.

Manuel, Peter, Latin America and the Caribbean, from *Popular Musics of the Non-Western World.* New York: Oxford University Press, 1988, pp. 24–83. Analyzes the different musical styles of Latin America and the Caribbean.

Roberts, John Storm, *Black Music of Two Worlds.* New York: Morrow Paperbacks, 1974. 282 p. A good introduction to black music in the African diaspora (Latin America, the Caribbean and the U.S.)

Journals
The Beat. Bi-monthly, formerly The Reggae and African Beat. "World beat" magazine covering popular music styles being recorded and performed around the world today (Bongo Productions, P.O. Box 29820, Los Angeles, CA., 90029).

De Lerma, Dominique-Rene, *Bibliography of Black Music, Vol 3: Geographical Studies.* Westport, CT. : Greenwood Press, 1982. See "The Southern Americas," pp. 164–193; "The Caribbean," pp. 127–163.

AFRO-BRAZILIAN SACRED AND FOLKLORIC MUSIC
Books and Articles
Andrade, Mario de, *Musica Feiticeira no Brasil.* Sao Paulo: Livraria Martins Editoria, 1962 (Portuguese text). Writings on the Afro-Brazilian cult music of the northeast of Brazil.

Bastide, Roger, *The African Religions of Brazil.* Baltimore: Johns Hopkins University Press, 1978. Explores the African religions of Brazil: Candomble, Umbanda, Batuque.

Behague, Gerard *Brazil: Folk Music,* from The New Grove Dictionary of Music and Musicians, Vol 3, pp. 221–244

Film
Berimbau (1971) Directed by Tony Talbot. (Distributed by New Yorker Films, 16 West 61st Street, New York NY 10023)

BRAZILIAN POPULAR MUSIC
Books and Articles
Barbosa, Orestes, *Samba: Sua Historia, Seus Poetas, Seus Musicos e Seus Cantores.* (Second edition, Portuguese text) Rio de Janeiro: Edicao Funarte, 1978. 125 p.

Gardel, Luis D., *Escolas De Samba: An Affectionate Descriptive Account of the Carnival Guilds of Rio de Janeiro.* Rio de Janeiro: Livraria Kosmos Editora, 1967. 200 p.

Marre, Jeremy and Hannah Charlton, *Spirit of Samba: The Black Music of Brazil.* From *Beats of the Heart: Popular Music of the World,* New York: Pantheon, 1986, pp. 215–228.

Muniz Jr., Jose, *Sambistas Importais: Dados Biograficos de 50 Figuras do Mundo do Samba.* Sao Paolo: Co-Edicao Impres, 1976 (Portuguese text).

Perrone, Charles A., *Masters of Contemporary Brazilian Song: MPB 1965-1985.* Austin: University of Texas Press, 1989. 253 p. An English-language study of some of Brazil's leading contemporary singer/songwriters and their music—Chico Buarque, Caetano Veloso, Gilberto Gil, Milton Nascimento, Joao Bosco, and Aldir Blanc.

Rocca, Edgard Nunes *Ritmos Brasileiros e Seus Instrumentos de Percussao.* Rio de Janeiro: Escola Brasileira de Musica/Europa-Empresa Grafica e Editora, 1986. 80 p. (Portuguese text).

Bibliographies
Brasil Musical–Brazil. A Journey through Popular Sounds and Rhythms, Art Bureau–Representacoes e Edicoes de Arte, 1988. In English and Portuguese, with a tape.

Perrone, Charles A., *An Annotated Inter-Disciplinary Bibliography and Discography of Brazilian Popular Music.* Latin American Music Review, Vol. 7. #2 (Fall–Winter 1986), pp. 302–340

Films and Videos
Black Orpheus Outstanding commercial film shot in the 1950's which includes numerous examples of batucada samba drumming and dancing as well as several bossa nova classics.

Carnaval '89 Magica e esplendor do major Carnaval do Mundo (The Magic and splendor of the greatest Carnival in the world). (Video) Manchete Video, bloch Producoes Ltda. Rua do Russell, 804. Telephone (021) 285-0033. Great footage of carnaval in Rio and other Brazilian cities.

Carnaval: The Force of Love and Kindness. Directed by Lyonel Lucine. 30 min. Behind-the-scenes view of one Rio de Janeiro community's involvement in the annual carnaval festivities. Includes scenes of preparing costumes and floats as well as samba school rehearsals leading up to the four-day event. Distributed by the Pennsylvania State University, Audio-Visual Services, Special Services Building, University Park, PA. 16802

Beats of the Heart: The Spirit of Samba–Black Music of Brazil (Video), Directed by Jeremy Marre. Includes Afro-Brazilian religious music, a Rio samba school, Gilberto Gil, Milton Nascimento, Chico Buarque and others.

Creation of the World: A Samba-Opera. Directed by Vera de Figueiredo. 56 min. Music and dance spectacular dramatizing the legend of Genesis according to the Yoruba mythology of Rio de Janeiro's black population. Sung and danced by members of the multi-award winning Beija Flor Samba School. (Distributed by the Cinema Guild, 1697 Broadway, Room 802, New York NY 10019)

For further information on videos containing information on Brazilian culture, contact the Caribbean Cultural Center (see Resource Centers).

Music Books and Articles
Sabavonich, Daniel, *Brazilian Percussion Manual: Rhythms and Techniques With Application for the Drumset*. Edited by Anthony J. Cirone. Alfred Publishing Co.1988. A well-presented manual on the batucada style used in the samba schools, as well as some interesting patterns for the drumset.

Moreira, Airto, *AIRTO, The Spirit of Percussion*. Edited by Rick Mattingly. 21st Century Music Productions, 1985. A good introduction to some of the main percussion instruments played in Brazilian music.

Gottlieb, Gordon, "The Percussion of Carnaval," from *Modern Percussionist* Magazine, Dec. 1984–Feb. 1985, pp. 12–17. A good presentation of the percussion instruments and parts played in the batucada style.

MAIL ORDER AND RECORD OUTLETS
Caravan Music, P.O. Box 49036, Austin TX 78765. Free mail-order catalogue with a strong Brazilian music section.

International Book and Record Distributors, 40-11 24th St., Long Island City NY 11101.

Original Music, R.D. #1, Box 190, Tivoli NY 12583; phone (914) 756-2767. Free mail-order catalogue.

RESOURCE CENTERS
Black Arts Research Center, 30 Marion St., Nyack NY 10960; phone (914) 358-2089. An archival resource center dedicated to the documentation, preservation and dissemination of the African cultural legacy, including records, cassettes, videotapes, books, journals and bibliographies.

Caribbean Cultural Center, 408 W. 58th St., New York NY 10019; phone (212) 307-7420. A non-profit organization dedicated to the study of African traditions in the arts and culture of the Caribbean, South America and the U.S. The center sponsors many excellent concerts of African-based folkloric music.

World Music Institute, 109 W. 27th St., New York NY 10011; phone (212) 545-7536. A non-profit organization which presents concerts in traditional and contemporary music from around the world. The Institute has a fine collection of records, tapes, CDs and literature on world music.